# THREE MIDDLE ENGLISH RELIGIOUS POEMS

Edited with an Introduction and Commentary

*by R. H. Bowers*

University of Florida Monographs

## HUMANITIES

No. 12, Winter 1963

UNIVERSITY OF FLORIDA PRESS / GAINESVILLE, FLORIDA

*PR*
*1203*
*B62*

---

46978

# PREFATORY NOTES

The Middle English texts transcribed in the following pages´ are preserved in apograph fair copies, apparently made by professional scribes during the early fifteenth century. There are few substantive errors; when they occur I have not hesitated to suggest an emendation and to record the MS reading in the notes. Contrary to the expensive editorial custom of the Early English Text Society editors, I have silently expanded obvious abbreviations; and introduced modern capitalization and punctuation — light rather than heavy. I see no point in attempting to reproduce the physical appearance of a medieval MS by using a variety of modern type fonts since photography alone will achieve such a result. The ME thorn has been transcribed by *th*; and the arabic numeral 3 has been used to designate the ME yogh. I have not tampered with the sometimes wayward syntax and erratic orthography of the numerous citations from Medieval Latin. Nor have I attempted to provide translations: (1) because such procedure would swell the body of the text and increase the cost of publication, and (2) because church Latin usually employs a fairly restricted vocabulary and is usually couched in straightforward cataphatic and apophatic declarations which pose no serious difficulty for the hardened medievalists who alone may read this monograph. I should add that all Vulgate citations, unless otherwise indicated, are made from the *Biblia Sacra juxta Vulgatam Clementinam* (Rome, 1947). Since it is virtually impossible to provide a commentary that will please all readers I offer no apology for my annotation. One either explains too much or too little; one is either irrelevant or pedantic.

It would hardly be feasible to try to thank all the good people who have helped me, directly or indirectly, in the preparation of this monograph: their names must be relegated to the notes, which is at once the fate and reward of scholarship. However I would like to make a few exceptions, since I know that my feelings about the literature and culture of late fourteenth century England have been nourished and enriched by the writings of Dom David Knowles, W. A. Pantin, Gordon Leff (especially his essay, "The Changing Pattern of Thought in the Earlier Fourteenth Century," *Bulletin of the John Rylands Library*, XLIII, 1961, 354-72), and Morton W. Bloomfield, whose recent *Piers Plowman as a Fourteenth Century Apocalypse* (New Brunswick, 1962) is a veritable encyclopaedia. And I have often had recourse to Millar Burrows, *An Outline of Biblical Theology* (Philadelphia, 1946).

I am greatly indebted to the Research Council of the University of Florida for a grant that enabled me to read both at the Cambridge University Library and at the British Museum during the summer of 1962, and hence to draw on hitherto unpublished manuscript material. During the past decade many libraries, such as the New York Public, the Newberry, the Library of Congress, and the Houghton Rare Book Library at Harvard, have tendered me hospitality. At home, the staff of the University of Florida Library has always shown me unfailing courtesy.

R.H.B.

# CONTENTS

*Le pécheur peut faire la meilleure prière.*
— Charles Péguy

# 1. INTRODUCTION

## THE MANUSCRIPTS

THIS monograph presents the texts of three hitherto unpublished anonymous late Middle English religious poems* which are preserved, uniquely it seems, in the following manuscripts.

### POEM 1

British Museum Royal MS 17.c.xvii, fol. 152ᵛ-155ᵛ.

"A newe lessoun Off Chrystys ressurrectoun." A pastoral legend in ME verse (249 couplets, with one triple end-rime on *ll.* 351-53) for the Resurrection of Christ, carrying the narrative on to Pentecost and concluding with an extended account of the Last Judgment.

Carleton Brown and Rossell H. Robbins, *The Index of Middle English Verse* (New York, 1943), No. 1189.

Incipit: Here begynnes a newe lessoun / Off Chrystys ressurrectoun.

See: Sir George F. Warner and Julius P. Gilson, A *Catalogue of the Western Manuscripts in the Old Royal and Kings' Collections* (London, 1921), II, 247. The MS is a miscellany of 24 separate grammatical and poetic items in Latin and Middle English, including texts of such works as Myrc's *Instructions for Parish Priests* and the *Life of Mary Magdalene* edited by Karl Horstmann for the Early English Text Society (OS No. 87, 1887). The MS is written on paper; consists of 116 folios in quarto, measuring 8¼ x 5½ inches; and belongs to the early fifteenth century.

### POEM 2

British Museum Additional MS 37,049, fol. 28ʳ.

*These poems illustrate and exemplify three major characteristics of the religious literature of the late fourteenth and fifteenth centuries in England: (1) a homiletic or pastoral purpose (cf. the ME *St. Bernard's Lamentation on Christ's Passion* (EETS OS No. 98, 1892, p. 298: "Lewed men be not lered in lore / As Clerkes ben in holi writ; / Thau3 men prechen hem bifore / Hit wol not wonen in heore wit"); (2) the reliance on Biblical material and commentary thereon, because: "Holi writ is oure myrour, / In whom we sen al vre socour" (*Speculum Gy de Warwyke*, EETS ES No. 75, 1898, *l.* 505); (3) the assumption of a devotional attitude and tone; cf. Hugh of St. Victor, *De Laude Charitatis* (Migne, *Patrologia Latina*, CLXXVI, 974): "Si Deus propter hominem tanta pertulit, quid homo propter Deum tolerare recusabit?"

1

A meditation on the Passion of Our Lord, consisting of 30 lines, 15 couplets.

Brown and Robbins, *Index*, No. 269.

Incipit: Also take hede to this insawmpyl here / That is lykend to the fawconere.

See: *A Catalogue of Additions to the Manuscripts in the British Museum in the Years* MDCCCC-MDCCCCV (London, 1907), p. 327. This MS, obtained from the Munich dealer Rosenthal in 1905, is one of the most important surviving miscellanies of ME religious pieces in prose and verse since it contains 71 separate items such as the ME *Desert of Religion*. Hope Emily Allen suggested (*Writings Ascribed to Richard Rolle*, New York, 1927, p. 307) that the MS might be of Carthusian origin since a ME poem on the founding of that order is contained therein. The MS has many vivid illustrations which Miss Allen considered crude and lurid, but which recent students have considered to be of more than passing interest; several of them have been reproduced: see Thomas W. Ross, "Five Fifteenth-Century 'Emblem' Verses," *Speculum*, XXXII (1957), 274-82; R. H. Bowers, "A Medieval Analogue to *As You Like It* II.vii.137-166," *SQ*, III (1952), 109-12. The MS is written on paper (which is now considerably browned); consists of 96 folios measuring 10¾ x 8 inches; and belongs to the first half of the fifteenth century.

## POEM 3

Cambridge University Library MS Dd.11.89, fol. 179ᵛ-185ᵛ.

A meditation on the Passion (400 lines in quatrains).

Brown and Robbins, *Index*, No. 2613.

Incipit: Of alle the ioyus that in this worlde may be.

See: C. Hartwick and H. R. Luard, *A Catalogue of the Manuscripts Preserved in the Library of the University of Cambridge* (Cambridge, 1856-67), II, 482. This MS is a small miscellany of 6 ME religious pieces, including texts of *The Abbey of the Holy Ghost*, *The Pricke of Conscience*, and *Guy of Warwick*. The catalogue gives as a full title for the piece being edited in this monograph: "How ich Cristenman owe for to hafe a remembraunce of the passion of our Lord Jesu Criste." The MS is written on parchment, in "seemingly different hands"; consists of 196 leaves in quarto; and belongs to the mid-fifteenth-century.

## FORM AND SUBJECT MATTER

The introduction of the *De Christo Crucifixo* attributed, perhaps in error, to John Scotus Erigena (c 810-877), reads as follows:

> *Hellenas Troasque suos cantaret Homerus,*
> *Romuleam prolem finxerat ipse Maro;*
> *At nos caeligenum regis pia facta canamus*
> *Continuo cursu quem canit orbis ovans.*[1]*

We have here, in a poem devoted to the central event of Christianity, the Crucifixion, a characteristic medieval assertion of the superiority of Christian to classical culture. Yet the author is anxious to let us know that he deems himself a sophisticated, educated man familiar with at least the identity of Homer and Vergil, and that he has attained some mastery of the language, rhetoric, and poetic appropriated from Roman antiquity by the Church — often with reluctant and mixed feelings.[2] Although this conviction of superiority permeates the bulk of medieval writing, it is properly subordinated to the fundamental Christian concern with the salvation of man.[3] Hence this body of literature is based primarily on the Bible, and is in effect an extended commentary thereon. The Bible was certainly the most studied book of the Middle Ages;[4] and most medieval literature treats a common fund of Biblical material and Catholic dogma.[5] Hence one finds constant and continual iteration of theme and topic — most evident in institutional creed and communal liturgy. But since the Bible is in actuality a library, comprised of many books by many different authors, replete with contradiction, paradox, philological and theological obscurity that defies ultimate comprehension, there seems to be no immediately foreseeable termination of Biblical scholarship.[6] Thus the study and consequent interpretation of the Bible in the Middle Ages, which is merely another way of describing the writing of medieval religious literature, shows constant and continual variation, especially among polemical and irenical writers, in both stylistic expression and theological interpretation of the common fund of Biblical materials. Significant variation, arising from fresh insight, is normally what interests us the most in both sacred and profane writing. There is scant variation or imagination evidenced in the three ME poems which are presented in this monograph. But they do touch on many themes and topics which are of

*Notes begin on page 11.

continuing interest to the student of the history of ideas as well as to the philologist.[7] These topics may be now listed.

## POEM 1

*a ll. 1-103*  The first poem starts with the *visitatio sepulchri* topic, the visit of the Three Maries to the sepulchre of Jesus.[8]

*b ll. 104-156*  The Five Appearances of Jesus after the Resurrection.[9]

*c ll. 164-189*  The Doubt of Thomas.[10]

*d ll. 190-206*  The Ascension.

*e ll. 207-218*  Prophecy by the Angels of the Parousia and the Last Judgment.

*f ll. 219-290*  Pentecost, the descent of the Holy Ghost on the Apostles, with the interpretative speech of Peter thereon.

*g ll. 291-413*  The Apostles, now endowed with charismatic power, instead of going forth to preach the kerygma ("et non est in alio aliquo salus"), deliver a homily on the terror of the Last Judgment and the need of prior repentance.[11]

*h ll. 414-442*  The Seven Deadly Sins.[12]

*i ll. 442-463*  The Blessed Virgin Mary as Mediatrix.[13]

*j ll. 464-502*  Preces (including a short description of the Joys of Heaven).

This summary shows that this devotional narrative contains a number of eschatological topics, but since the main emphasis falls on the Doomsday, or Last Judgment, topic, one could find justification for calling the poem a Doomsday poem. Or, from another point of view, the poem could be called a "Biblical-creed-narrative" prayer, since all these ingredients are present: this genre was fairly common in France, and may be found throughout medieval Christendom; see Sister Marie Pierre Koch, *Analysis of the Long Prayers in Old French Literature with Special Reference to the Biblical-Creed-Narrative Prayers* (Washington, D. C., 1940).

## POEM 2

*a ll. 1-6*  The second poem starts with a similitude drawn from falconry, comparing a hawk recalled by a lure to the penitent turning to the lure of Christ crucified.

*b ll. 6-30*  Self-crucifixion of the penitent, passing by degrees from sympathy to empathy, characteristic of Franciscan devotion, and suggesting the legend that St. Francis in the solitude of Mount Alvernus received the stigmata.

4

## POEM 3

*a ll. 1-59*   Proem: the third poem starts with an assertion of the advantages of loving God, of meditation on the Passion.[14]

*b ll. 57-184*   An account of the Passion.[15]

*c ll. 185-200*   The Anguish of Mary.

*d ll. 225-244*   Christ as the Good Shepherd.

*e ll. 257-280*   The Legend of Longinus.[16]

*f ll. 289-327*   Planctus Mariae.

*g ll. 323-402*   Preces.

These poems are clearly designed to stimulate the indifferent[17] to repentance and a renewal of Christian piety, and were composed presumably by clerics or men in orders who felt authorized to perform such an office.[18] They can therefore be called homiletic or pastoral poems designed to save men's souls; and although they are not tightly organized one can see a building through the sequence of material to a rhetorical epitasis of prayer.[19] They are written in English rather than in Latin, presumably to appeal to a lay audience. They are written in verse rather than in the patterned prose which became increasingly popular as a devotional medium towards the end of the fourteenth century in England.[20] But perhaps the most important thing to notice about these poems is that they treat a number of different topics. Any ME devotional work of more than lyric length is apt to plait or stitch clumsily many themes and motives with a homiletic and monitory emphasis that provides coherence and unity of tone and purpose.[21] Some ME devotional manuals concerned primarily with "perfecting" ascending degrees of contemplation — the stages of purification, illumination, and unification, such as the anonymous ME *Cloud of Unknowing*, also provide didactic teaching of the usual moral kind found in the medieval sermon. *The Mirror of Holy Church (Speculum Ecclesiae)*[22] of St. Edmund, Archbishop of Canterbury (d. 1240),[23] a most influential work, sets forth conventional homiletic doctrine as well as vivid meditations on the Passion. The theme of the *Mirror* is the three kinds of knowledge of God: (1) through contemplation of God in His creatures and in the created universe; (2) through contemplation of God in Holy Writ, which instructs us in such matters as the Ten Commandments, the Seven Gifts of the Holy Ghost, and so forth; and (3) through the contemplation of God in His Manhood, for which St. Edmund devises divine meditations on significant scenes in the ministry of Christ, and especially in the Passion.

Thus classification of ME religious literature is difficult, and often is at best arbitrary. Recently W. A. Pantin has refined the classifications used in older handbooks, as that of J. E. Wells, *A Manual of the Writings in Middle English* (New Haven, 1916).[24] He proposes three main categories, arising from three different cultural and institutional forces: (1) manuals of instruction for parish priests, arising from the disciplinary legislation and program of the Church; (2) technical treatises ("summae," "specula") of moral and pastoral theology describing the vices and virtues, intended primarily for the laity; (3) mystical literature and lyrics of devotion, concentrated on the Person and Name of Jesus, stimulated by Cistercian and Franciscan piety. One might propose other categories, such as the Biblical narrative exemplified by the ME *Cursor Mundi* and the ME *Stanzaic Life of Christ* which involve the intricate problem of harmonizing the contradictory accounts of the life of Our Lord as testified to in the Synoptic Gospels and the Fourth Gospel.[25] One might further propose categories for drama, hagiography, or sermon. But again the significant fact to observe is that these proposed categories are not mutually exclusive since they may all be permeated by, and hence linked with, homiletic purposes and monitory assertions; and they all draw on a common store of Biblical and dogmatic material. Finally, if one accepts the description of Christianity as being essentially missionary in spirit, one can say that these ME writings carry on this noble mission.

The great eschatological topics of the Passion and of the Last Judgment receive major emphasis in the three ME poems in this monograph. They are central topics which find continual expression in the services of the Church and in the literature and thought of the faithful. They have been pondered and interpreted by generations of theologians. And they have received different emphasis in different periods of history, a brief account of which will now occupy the subsequent paragraphs.

Half a century ago the great French historian of church iconography, Émile Mâle, drawing his unassailable evidence and illustration from the visible decorations of the great French medieval cathedrals, charted a major shift in cultural sensibility in the West. During the twelfth and thirteenth centuries Jesus is depicted as a stern judge in the representations of "le jugement dernier," or as a calm, benign teacher, as at Amiens or Bourges; but in the fourteenth century He is depicted as Christ crucified, as a man who has suffered all of man's inhumanity to man, as the Redeemer, as the "vir dolorum et sciens infirmitatem." During the earlier period the deserved suffering of the damned is stressed, as at Laon or Bordeaux; during the later period the suffering of Jesus is stressed, with poignant realism of detail designed to move the common man. Mâle writes: "Jésus n'enseigne plus, il souffre: ou plutôt il semble nous proposer ses plaies et son sang comme l'enseignement suprême."[26] The shift, in other words, is from concern with the topic of the Last Judgment to the topic of the Passion, from judgment to redemption, from justice to mercy, although, as we shall see, the newer sensibility never ousted the older from consideration in the devotional and homiletic literature of the late Middle Ages in England.

The concept of Jesus is entirely different in the two topics: Jesus as the stern judge and Jesus as the loving redeemer. When placed in abrupt juxtaposition the contrast is striking.

In the ME *York* Judgment pageant, which has been considered the best of the four judgment plays in the ME Corpus Christi cycles by both J. Q. Adams (*Chief Pre-Shakespearian Dramas*, Boston, 1924) and A. C. Cawley (*Everyman and Medieval Miracle Plays*, New York, 1959) in their assembling of the best dramatic illustrations from the cycles, Jesus judges the sinners harshly:

> Ye cursid caytiffs of Kaymes kynne   (i.e., Cain's)
> That neuer me comforte in my care,
> I and ye for-euer will twynne
> In dole to dwelle for-euermare.   (*ll.* 317-20)

One of the sinners goes so far as to despair of redemption (the text does not make clear whether the sinner is in a state of wanhope, which is a sin against the Holy Ghost since it despairs of the mercy of God):

> We mon be sette for our synnes sake
> For-euere fro oure saluacioune,
> In helle to dwelle with feendes blake,
> Wher neuer schall be redempcioune.   (*ll.* 141-44)

In *Piers Plowman* Christ is represented as the loving redeemer when He states after the Harrowing of Hell and the consequent redemption of the sinful:

7

For I, that am lorde of lyf. loue is my drynke,
And for that drynke to-day. I deyde upon erthe.
I faughte so, me threstes yet. for mannes soule sake;
May no drynke me moiste. ne my thruste slake,
Tyl the vendage falle. in the vale of Iosephath,
That I drynke righte ripe must. *resureccio mortuorum,*
And thanne shal I come as a kynge. crouned with angeles,
And han out of helle, alle mennes soules.     (B.XVIII.363-70)

Yet the York play is perfectly orthodox: the "cursid caytiffs" trans-
lates the "maledicti" of Matthew xxv, 42: "Discedite a me maledicti
in ignem aeternum." The Doomsday topic is wholly orthodox: based
almost literally on Matthew xxv, 31-46, it constitutes a central point
of Christian eschatology and is proclaimed as Article vii of the
Apostles' Creed, sanctioned in the *De Fide Catholica* of the Fourth
Lateran Council of 1251,[27] and embodied in one of the most famous
hymns of the Middle Ages, the "Dies Irae," where Jesus is addressed
as "Juste judex ultionis."[28] It is likewise an article of the Anglican
faith: John Pearson, Bishop of Chester, in his *An Exposition of the
Creed* (1659), says of the Seventh Article, "He shall come to judge
the quick and the dead," that belief therein "prevents *dangerous
doubts* [my italics] rising against the ruling of the World by the
Providence of God."[29]

The Doomsday topic was such a favorite theme in Old English
Christian poetry that it was often inserted in poems dealing with
other subjects.[30] Possibly the best OE treatment of the topic is to be
found in *Be Domes Daeʒe* (a rendition of Bede's *De Die Iudicii*),
with its vivid depiction of the horrors of hell and the joys of heaven.[31]
The topic continued to attract English writers throughout the centuries: as mentioned above, the York, Chester, Coventry, and Towneley dramatic cycles all have Judgment Day pageants, one of the most
popular ME poems, *The Pricke of Conscience* (which survives in
over 100 MSS), develops the topic in minute detail, and continual
citations may be observed, as in a ME sermon from Royal MS
18.B.xxiii: "The synneful men in ignem eternum et iusti in vitam
eternam."[32] The significant aspect of the Last Judgment topic resides
in its stress on retributive justice—not on mercy. The love and mercy
of Mark ii, 17: "Non necesse habent sani medico, sed qui male
habent; non enim veni vocare justos sed peccatores"; of Romans v, 8:
"Commendat autem charitatem suam Deus in nobis, quoniam cum
adhuc peccatores essemus, secundum tempus Christus pro nobis

mortuus est," are overshadowed by the stern declaration of Revelation xix, 11: that God "cum justitia judicat." No doubt it would be a gross overstatement to argue that the tone and orientation of the religious life in England in the early Middle Ages, as set forth in the surviving religious documents and monuments, was ridden with fear and terror of the Last Judgment. Yet an inordinate stress does seem to be placed on the necessary intercession of good angels and saints to plead for the miserable sinner: "Deus qui miro ordine angelorum ministeria hominumque dispenses, concede propitius, ut, quibus tibi ministrantibus in coelo semper adsistitur, ab his in terra, nostra vita muniamur."[33]

The newer sensibility of devotion to the Passion, or Christocentric piety as it is often called by recent scholars, is usually associated in the textbooks with the Franciscans (the motto of their order is "Mihi absit gloriari nisi in cruce Domini"). Actually the sensibility appears to have been first clearly expressed by Anselm and Damiani, and to have been elaborated in loving detail by St. Bernard, yet the Franciscans, especially Bonaventura, made the Passion the center of everything, of their theology, art and devotion.[34] Hope Emily Allen has noted that at the time of Rolle, whose ME *Meditations on the Passion* is sometimes regarded as the most beautifully written ME example of this genre, the *Meditationes Vitae Christi* and the *Stimulus Amoris* (both once attributed, perhaps dubiously, to Bonaventura) "were the great storehouses of imaginative narrative founded on the Gospels from which medieval devotion fed its ardour and its fancy."[35] The *Meditationes* enlarge the bare outlines of canonical narrative, invent and invest new scenes of the Passion with lively color and concrete detail, elaborate the anguish of Mary, enlarge the hyperdulia of the "mater dolorosa," pass over dogma in order to represent a personal and poignant human experience for the pius to contemplate.[36] The fascinating ME *Boke of Margery Kempe* records of that excitable mystic that:

Whan sche was ther [in the priory cloister of St. Margaret's, Lynn], sche had so gret mende of the Passyon of owr Lord Ihesu Crist & of hys precyows wowndys & how dere he bowt hir that sche cryed & roryed wondirfully so that sche myth be herd a gret way & myth not restreyne hyr-self therfro. Than had sche gret wondyr how owı Lady myth suffyr er dur to see hys precyows body ben scorgyd & hangyd on the Crosse. Also it cam to hir mende how men had seyd to hir-self be-forn that owr Lady, Cristys owyn Modyr, cryed not as

9

sche dede, & that cawsyd hir to seyn in hir crying, "Lord, I am not thi modir. Take a-way this peyn fro me, for I may not beryn it. Thi Passyon wil sle me." So ther cam a worschepful clerk forby hir, a doctowr of diuinite & sade, "I had leuyr than xx pownde that I myth han swech a sorwe for owr Lordys Passyon."[37]

Two great traditions mark the gradual shift in medieval sensibility from emphasis on the terror of the Last Judgment to hope for the mercy and the redemption afforded by the Passion.[38] The first tradition consists of the gradual elevation of the Blessed Virgin Mary to the role of mediator for sinful man ("fac sit nobis iudex placabilis, o Maria"), and later to the theologically strained role of co-redemptress;[39] the second tradition is the remarkable allegory of the Four Daughters of God. The first tradition, proclaimed in the majestic hymn, "Stabat Mater Dolorosa," has been explained at a popular level in the following words: "Only by recourse to a woman's pity could the medieval imagination find a hope of robbing the terrible Day of Judgment of part at least of that terror which pressed so heavily upon the soul."[40] Sister Mary Vincentine Gripkey, in her comprehensive *The Blessed Virgin Mary as Mediatrix in the Latin and Old French Legend prior to the Fourteenth Century* (Washington, 1938), has surveyed the growth of the tradition in the literature. An interesting addition may be adduced from icongraphy: one figura has St. Michael holding the scales of judgment while the Virgin Mary and St. John plead for the sinner (south façade of Chartres);[41] Daniel Rock illustrates an English rendition wherein St. Michael holds a golden balance with a quaking soul in one scale and a hairy devil in the other as the Blessed Virgin casts a rosary into the scale holding the quaking soul and tips the balance.[42] That spacious compendium of legend, the *Legenda Aurea* of the Dominican Provincial of Lombardy, Jacobus de Voragine (d. 1298), tells a similar story: "A certain sinner had a vision that he was claimed by the Devil before the Judgment seat of God. Truth and Justice urged him to have recourse to the Mother of Mercy who sits beside the Lord, and earnestly call forth her aid. And when he did so, the Blessed Mary came to his aid, and laid her hand on the side of the balance wherein were the few good deeds, while the Devil struggled to pull down the other side; but the Mother of Mercy prevailed, and won the sinner's freedom. Whereupon he returned to himself, and thenceforth led a better life."[43]

The second tradition is the allegory of the Four Daughters of God,

10

which is represented in a fully developed form in such ME works as *Piers Plowman*, Lydgate's *Life of Our Lady*, and *The Court of Sapience*. It may be briefly summarized as follows: After the disobedience of Adam, the destiny of postlapsarian man is debated between God's Justice and Truth, who demand legalistic satisfaction, and His Mercy and Peace, who urge forgiveness. The opposing principles, debated at length in long oratorical set-pieces in the Parliament of Heaven, are reconciled only when the Son offers Himself as a redeeming Sacrifice for sinful man who is unable, by himself, to provide satisfaction. The nucleus of the theme is to be found in Psalm lxxxiv, 11: "Misericordia et veritas obviaverunt sibi; justitia et pax osculatae sunt."[44] The theme exemplifies the perpetual debate between justice and mercy which has engaged human society in the West throughout the ages – it can almost be said to pose an insoluble dilemma.[45] It intrudes itself forcefully into the agonizing dilemma that complicates the administration of modern penal institutions: is the criminal sick or guilty? is he responsible for his actions, or irresponsible because of a faulty upbringing, or because of extraneous circumstances over which he has had no effective control?

In summation, then, we may say that the pleading of the Blessed Virgin Mary, the pleading of Mercy and Peace, audibly voice the medieval sentiment that protested against the legalism, the retributive justice of the Last Judgment. But the greatest consolation is derived from the reassurance of the Passion tradition that "Christus passus est pro nobis.[46]

## NOTES

1. *PL.* CXXII, 1221.
2. The competitive persistence of classical letters and culture during the Middle Ages is a vast subject; a few general surveys addressed to its description may be cited: M. Roger, *L'Enseignement des lettres classiques d'Ausone à Alcuin* (Paris, 1905); Dom Jean Leclerq, *L'Amour des lettres et le désir de Dieu: Initiation aux auteurs monastiques du moyen âge* (Paris, 1957); Ernst R. Curtius, *Europäische Literatur und Lateinisches Mittelalter* (Bern, 1948); Jean Seznec, *The Survival of the Pagan Gods* (New York, 1954); Beryl Smalley, *English Friars and Antiquity* (Oxford, 1960); G. Paré, A. Brunet, P. Tremblay, *La Renaissance du XIIe Siècle: Les écoles et l'enseignement* (Paris, 1933).
3. When religious sentiment and imagination is a dominant force in a given civilization its influence is shown throughout even avowedly secular literature: for Christian coloring in the ME metrical romances, see Mother Mary Nobert, *The Reflection of Religion in English Medieval Verse Romances* (Bryn Mawr, 1941); Albert C. Baugh, "The Authorship of the ME Romances," *Annual Bulletin of the Modern Humanities Research Association*, No. xxii (1950), 13-28.

4. See Beryl Smalley, *The Study of the Bible in the Middle Ages* (2nd ed.; Oxford, 1952), p. xi.

5. Religious literature has a sanctified substance wholly apart from the mere words or rhetoric in which it is expressed: form is never confused with content, as it is by many misguided modern critics; of Rabanus Maurus, *De Clericorum Institutione* (PL, CVII, 408): "Est autem optimus modus dicendi, qui fit ut qui audit, verum audiat; et quae audit, intelligat; bonorumque ingeniorum insignis est indoles; in verbis verum amare, non verba." It was often argued that the Holy Ghost sanctified the utterances of preachers enlarging on Holy Writ, or the exegesis of Biblical commentators, as persons dealing with "real things." T. M. Charland, *Artes Praedicandi* (Paris, 1936), p. 8, refers to "L'éloquence religieuse ou le Saint Esprit lui-même doit être l'inspirateur"; P. C. Spicq, *Esquisse d'une histoire de l'exégèse latine* (Paris, 1944), p. 373, states that, on the authority derived from I Cor. xii, "L'interpretation des paroles est comptée parmi les autre dons du Saint-Esprit." Henri de Lubac, S.J., *Exégèse médiévale* (Aubier, 1959), I.ii.522-23, remarks on "la connaissance du Christ puisée dans l'Écriture."

6. James D. Smart, *The Interpretation of Scripture* (Philadelphia, c 1961), p. 13, observes that "The history of Biblical interpretation is the story of how the Church has over and over again to rediscover the Scriptures." Medieval complaints about the difficulty of Biblical interpretation are commonplace: e.g., Richard de Bury (or Robert Holcot?), *Philobiblon*, Kings' Classics ed.; London 1902), cap. v, p. 41. However the objection: "paucis penetrabilis est Scriptura quia obscura est et quasi clausa," could be readily countered by any ready theologian by citing from his vade mecum, Augustine's *De Doctrina Christiana*, such an assertion as: "Nihil enim fere de illis eruitur, quod non planissime dictum alibi reperiatur" (II, vi; PL, XXXIV, 39).

7. Étienne Gilson once accused the savant Gaston Paris of being "indifferent to ideas," of managing "to combine with a most exacting scientific rigour about what the medievals wrote, a perfectly unscrupulous arbitrariness about what they thought" (*The Spirit of Medieval Philosophy*, New York, 1936, p. 384). Happily this situation is changing for the better as the decades pass; it is hard to conceive of a scholar being a good philologist who lacks an informed awareness of the history of ideas. A good statement of the proper role of the history of ideas in literary scholarship is made by R. S. Crane, "Literature, Philosophy, and the History of Ideas," MP, LII (1954-55), 80 ff. The history of ideas often exploits second-rate literature; hence from early times editors of ME texts have often felt somewhat apologetic for the fare they were offering their readers: in 1652 Elias Ashmole prefaced his miscellany of ME alchemical tracts (*Theatrum Chemicum Britannicum*) with the following remarks: "The style and language thereof, may, I confesse (to some) seeme Irksome and Uncouth, and so it is indeed to those that are strangers thereunto; but withall very significant; old words have strong emphasis; others may look on them as Rubbish or Trifles, but they are grosly mistaken: for what some light braines may esteem as foolish toys; deeper judgements can and will value as sound and serious matter" (sig. B4r).

8. This topic forms the genesis of the medieval drama; see Karl Young, *The Drama of the Medieval Church* (Oxford, 1933), II, 606, s.v. "Visitatio Sepulchri."

9. For this topic see Jean G. Wright, *A Study of the Themes of the Resurrection in the Medieval French Drama* (Bryn Mawr, 1935), chap. vi.

10. For this topic see Eleanor Prosser, *Drama and Religion in the English Mystery Plays* (Stanford, Calif., 1961), esp. pp. 147-78.

11. The ME *Cursor Mundi*, the great Biblical narrative which absorbs the

traditions of Peter Comestor's *Historia Scholastica* and the pseudo-Strabo *Glossa Ordinaria*, properly has the apostles preaching the Gospel : "In their spelling, ful wele thai sped" (*EETS OS* No. 66. 1887, *l.* 19200); for modern commentary see C. S. C. Williams, *A Comentary on the Acts of the Apostles* (New York, 1957), pp. 82-83. For ME poems which conflate the topic of the formulation of the Apostle's Creed with the traditions of the *Actus Apostolorum* and the hagiography of the careers of the apostles themselves, see R. H. Bowers, "Three Middle English Poems on the Apostles' Creed," *PMLA*, LXX (1955), 210-22.

12. The standard treatment of this topic is by Morton W. Bloomfield, *The Seven Deadly Sins* (East Lansing, Mich., 1952).

13. See Sister Mary Vincentine Gripkey, *The Blessed Virgin Mary as Mediatrix in the Latin and Old French Legend prior to the Fourteenth Century* (Washington, 1938); Joannes Vriend, S.J., *The Blessed Virgin Mary in the Medieval Drama of England* (Purmerend, Holland, 1928); Brother Luke Cornelius, *The Rôle of the Virgin Mary in the Coventry, York, Chester, and Towneley Cycles* (Washington, 1933).

14. Meditations on the Passion, following the tradition of "Bonaventura," usually tabulate a list of the advantages which accrue therefrom. The medieval love of drawing copious distinctions, degrees, and definitions is illustrated by:

Heir follows the xii fruttis that cumis of the remembrance of the passion of Crist:
The first is turnyng fra syne to vertu.
The secound, Crist makis a vertuis man of a vicius.
The thrit, Crist makis peace betuix the fader of hevin and that man.
The ferd, all aduersite is lycht to that man.
The fift, God schawis his will to that man.
The sext, God gevis deuocioun & with that heris his orison.
The sevint, that man is writtin in the partis in Cristis body, that is, in his hedde till help him, in his feit to byid with him, in his hart to think on him.
The viii: meditacion of the passion excedis vthir gud werkis.
For Albert sayis continuall & deuoit meditation of the passioun is better na to fast a yer bred & watter, & daly scurge him self quhill the blude ryn our, or daly reid a psalter.
The ix: suppois all haly kirk pray for a man, he may get mair grace him self for remembring of the passion.
The tent: deuoit remembrance of the passion is better than our Lady & all the sanctis prayit for him. The xi: & a man haue levit ill syn efter remembris devoitly of the passion he wynnis mair merit than ane uthir that hes nocht sa gret remembrance, suppois he haue levit weill. The xii: in his ded he gettis eternall consolacioun & bliss. Euery day of the euk hes a part of this exercicion becaus a day is our littil. (J. A. W. Bennett, *Devotional Pieces in Verse and Prose from MS Arundel 285 and MS Harleian 6919, Scottish Text Society*, 3rd Series, XXIII, 1955, 213/23.)

Many similar statements may be cited: the following short ME poem, hitherto unprinted (from British Museum MS Additional 37,049: Brown & Robbins, *Index*, No. 4140), is of interest because it shows an awareness of German Dominican piety:

Whoso rememors Cristes passion deuoutely
    To hym profets specially two thinges in hye:
The tone is if a man be put in heuynes
    It remefes away his gret distres;

13

> Also ane other it dos & helps certanly
>    To relese the bitter paynes of purgatory.
> This affermes the boke *Horologium Sapiencie* cald
> To thaim that deuoutely Cristes passion in mynde wil halde. (fol. 28ᵛ)

(An allusion to the *Horologium Sapientiae* of Henricus Suso, the great Dominican mystic of Ulm who died in 1366, and who is accorded a sympathetic estimation in J. M. Clark, *The Great German Mystics: Eckhardt, Tauler and Suso* [Oxford, 1949]. A ME version of this work is preserved in Douce MS 114, and was edited by Horstmann in *Anglia*, X, 1888, 357 ff; a French text is preserved in Harley MS 4386. The work was frequently printed in the fifteenth century in response to the great demand at that time for spiritual literature noted by E. P. Goldschmidt, *Medieval Texts and Their First Appearance in Print* [London, 1943], p. 51; Stillwell, Nos. S-773-77. In 1491 Caxton printed a version under the title *The Booke of divers ghostly matters*, STC 3305.)

Finally, it should be noted that the events of the Passion often became arranged according to canonical hours and thus established the Hours of the Cross tradition: e.g., the ME *Poems of John Audelay* (EETS OS No. 184, 1931), No. 14: "Hic incepiunt hore canonice passionis Ihesu Christe," which ends:

> He that these ours wil say with deuocion
> In reuerens and worchip of Crist passion,
> And schryue him clen to a prest with contricion
> God He grauntis him of His grace ful remyssion
>      Of al his trespace.      (ll. 82-86)

15. See Sister John Sullivan, A *Study of the Themes of the Sacred Passion in the Medieval Cycle Plays* (Washington, 1943); Frances A. Foster in her introduction to *The Northern Passion* (EETS OS No. 147, 1916), pp. 47-80.

16. The older dissertation of Rose J. Peeples, *The Legend of Longinus in Ecclesiastical Tradition and in English Literature* (Baltimore, 1911), needs to be supplemented; see further Jean G. Wright (*op. cit.*), pp. 1-23; Konrad Burdach, "Der Longinusspeer in eschatologischen Lichte," in his collected papers, *Vorspiel* (Halle, 1925), I, 217-52.

17. I prefer the term "indifferent" to F. M. Powicke's term "pagan" for those Catholics who were in a "state of acquiescence" but who were not "hostile to, though easily wearied by, religious observance" (art., "The Christian Life," in *The Legacy of the Middle Ages*, ed. C. G. Crump and E. F. Jacob, Oxford, 1926, p. 30). Persons of divided mind, who sought belief or righteousness and could not find it, were perhaps greater in number than historians imagine; a famous example of this tendency is the story of the father of the epileptic child cured by Jesus in Mark ix, 20-24: "Jesus autem ait illi. Si potes credere, omnia possibilia sunt credenti. Et continuo exclamans pater pueri, cum lacrymis aiebat: Credo, Domine; adjuva incredulitatem meam."

18. William Langland, if he be the author of *Piers Plowman*, calls such authors "correctors" (B.x.284), and then, with characteristic irony, says: "corecteth fyrst ʒow-seluen." England had a long tradition of rules, part disciplinary, part devotional, composed for recluses, such as the *Advice to Recluses* in Harley MS 2372, which started with Ailred's *Regula Inclusarum* (PL, XXXII, 1451 ff.).

19. See the fundamental articles of Rossell H. Robbins, "Popular Prayers in ME Verse," *MP*, XXXVI (1938), 337-50; "Private Prayers in ME Verse," *SP*, XXXVI (1939), 467-75.

20. Many medieval instructional works which today might be written in prose were written in verse, often for mnemonic reasons; see lists in Migne, *PL*, CCI, 86, s.v. "poesis didactica"; for ME sermons in verse, see G. R. Owst, *Preaching*

*in Medieval England* (Cambridge, 1926), pp. 271-78. Protests against the vanity of versification, urged by puritan sentiment, should also be noted: many examples from monastic sources are assembled by Dom Jean Leclerq (*op. cit.*, p. 172); furthermore, St. Edmund disliked rimed, apparently mnemonic, versions of the Pater Noster "for God him-self made hit; and therefor he doth gret schome and gret vnreurrence to God that taketh him to rymede wordes and queynts, and leueth the wordes and the preyere that he vs tauhte...." (*Mirror of Holy Church*, in Horstmann, *Yorkshire Writers*, II, 251); Wyclif disliked preachers who resorted to rime: "thei docken Goddis word and tateren it be ther rimes" (*Select English Works*, ed. T. Arnold, Oxford, 1869-71, III, 180). Related is the persistent puritan suspicion of poetry itself and the consequent effort of the poet to justify his practice and attain honorific status; see Hans Glunz, *Die Literaturästhetik des europäischen Mittelalters* (Bochum-Langendreer, 1937); and R. B. McKeon, "Rhetoric during the Middle Ages," *Speculum*, XVIII (1942), 1-32.

21. Compare the observations of Charlotte D'Evelyn on the ME *Meditations on the Life and Passion of Christ* (EETS OS No. 158, 1921), pp. xv-xvi: "There is no one guiding thread running throughout the poem. The events which form the subject of the meditations are often introduced out of their chronological order...." This feature is likewise characteristic of a good deal of profane literature: Curt F. Bühler states of the ME *Court of Sapience* that "it is little more than a literary mosaic. The author has gathered together from numerous sources a vast quantity of information, and his poem represents him as a scholar rather than as a poet" (*The Sources of the Court of Sapience* [Beiträge zur Englischen Philologie, xxiii], Leipzig, 1932, p. 17).

22. On the term "speculum," see Sister Ritamary Bradley, "Backgrounds of the Title Speculum in Medieval Literature," *Speculum*, XXIX (1954), 100-115. The Elizabethans used such terms as "mirror," "glass," or "anatomy."

23. For a sympathetic account of St. Edmund, see A. B. Emden, *An Oxford Hall in Medieval Times: Being the Early History of St. Edmund's Hall* (Oxford, 1927), pp. 81-104.

24. See W. A. Pantin, *The English Church in the XIV Century* (Cambridge, 1955), pp. 189 ff.

25. Reflecting, perhaps, views that would be shared by other modern exegetes, Morton S. Enslin declares that the effort to produce a harmony of the four Gospels "is utterly perverse and cannot fail to result in complete confusion," because 90 per cent of the material of the Gospel of John falls outside the Synoptic tradition (*The Literature of the Christian Movement*, New York, 1938, p. 437). Obviously the poets appearing in this monograph were not troubled by such a caveat.

26. *L'Art religieux de la fin du moyen âge* (Paris, 1925), p. 86; see also Louis Brehier, *L'Art chrétien* (Paris, 1928), pp. 308 ff; Joseph de Borchgrave d'Altena, *La passion du Christ dans la sculpture en Belgique du XIe au XVIe siècles* (Bruxelles, 1946).

27. H. Denzinger, *Enchiridion Symbolorum* (23rd ed.; Freiburg im Breisgau, 1937), No. 429: "venturus in fine saeculi, iudicaturus vivos et mortuos, et redditurus singulis secundum opera sua, tam reprobis quam electis . . . ut recipiant secundum opera sua sive bona fuerint sive mala illi cum diaboli poenam perpetuam et isti cum Christo gloriam sepiternam."

28. The "Dies Irae" is at bottom a prayer for the remission of sin, an urgent desire to escape the filth of the flesh: "Juste judex ultionis / Donum fac remissionis / Ante diem rationis" (*Roman Missal*, ed. Abbot Cabrol, O.S.B., New York, 1934, p. 1352). This is the usual request of medieval prayer; e.g.: "Lord,

haue merci on my synne / And brynge me out of al my care" (Carleton Brown, *Religious Lyrics of the XIVth Century*, Oxford, 1924, p. 121).

29. Cited from the 4th ed., London, 1676, p. 304. This view seems to be typical of the administrative official who tends, almost by instinct, to employ both physical and psychological coercion, the surds in idealistic political theory, to maintain the established social order. Cf. the irritation of another administrator, Innocent III, with the schoolmasters' incessant quibbling about transubstantiation: "subtiliter magis quam utiliter possent inquiri" (*PL*, CCXVII, 870).

30. See Charles W. Kennedy, *Early English Christian Poetry* (New York, 1952), p. 251; Walter Deering, *The Anglo-Saxon Poets on the Judgment Day* (Halle, 1890), carefully described the OE poetic treatment of the topic.

31. *EETS OS* No. 65 (1876).

32. *Middle English Sermons* (*EETS OS* No. 209, 1940), p. 318.

33. *Rituale Eccl. Dunelmensis*, cited by Daniel Rock, *The Church of Our Fathers*, ed. G. W. Hart and W. H. Frere (London, 1905), III, 71.

34. See R. W. Southern, *The Making of the Middle Ages* (London, 1953), pp. 218 ff.; É Gilson, "S. Bonaventure et l'iconographie de la Passion," *Revue d'histoire Franciscaine*, I (1924), 405 ff.; P. Pourrat, *La spiritualité chrétienne* (Paris, 1946), II i; Erich Auerbach, *Mimesis* (Princeton, 1953), pp. 162-73, on Franciscan expression. It is important to note that there must have been considerable opposition to the development of the Passion tradition, especially among literal-minded traditionalists. Gilbert Crispin's *Disputatio Judaei cum Christiano* (*PL*, CLIX, 1034) represents a fictitious Jewish spokesman who is shocked at the inconographic depiction of Christ cruicified, at the humanization of a divine personage, at the presumed violation of the law of Exodus xx, 4: "Non facies tibi sculptile." The Jew says: "quia et Christiani adorant sculptilia ... ipsum etenim Deum effigiatis aliquando miserum pendentem in patibulo cruci, clavis affixum, quod ipso etiam visu horrendum est." It might be argued that Crispin is here merely using the rhetorical maneuver of introducing a straw man or hypothetical position in order to enable his Christian spokesman to defend the Passion tradition *con brio*; but it is more than likely that a contemporary difference of opinion is being reflected. And it would not be gratuitous to add that at a later date in England the Puritans often rejected the related doctrine of vicarious atonement (n.b., John Milton), or interpreted the Atonement as the appointment of the elect to "join with Christ in the war against the eternal enemy. Thus the symbolism of the nativity and the passion came to mean little to the Puritan saints, and Christmas and Easter faded from their calendar" (William Haller, *The Rise of Puritanism*, New York, 1938, pp. 150-51).

35. See *English Writings of Richard Rolle*, ed. Hope Emily Allen (Oxford, 1951), p. 18. Walter Hilton translated the *Stimulus Amoris*, a modernized version of which was edited by Clare Kirchberger (London, 1952) under the title *The Goad of Love*.

36. Several ME recensions of "Bonaventura" were made: one under the title *The Privity of the Passion* is available in Horstmann, *Yorkshire Writers*, I, 198-218; Nicholas Love's version was edited by L. F. Powell (Oxford, 1911), under the title *The Mirrour of the Blessed Lyf of iesu Crist*. See also *PMLA*, XL (1925), 249 ff.

37. *EETS OS* No. 212 (1940), p. 164/16-30.

38. R. W. Southern (*op. cit.*, pp. 219-56), in a perceptive chapter entitled "From Epic to Romance," sees the development of the Passion tradition as articulated mainly by Anselm and Bernard, and as marking a great shift in the West from communal to individual sensibility, from the Theocentric to the Christocentric, from the static to the dynamic. Although Southern does not dis-

cuss it, the ubiquitous legend of the Harrowing of Hell (for an account of which see the Introduction to *EETS ES* No. 50, 1907) would reflect the older tradition of the Devil's abuse of power (see Timothy Fry, O.S.B., "The Unity of the *Ludus Coventriae*," *SP*, XLVIII, 1951, 529-32). Briefly, this theory holds that as a result of Original Sin, Satan had the legal right to inflict death on all mankind and hold them captive in hell. But Christ was not subject to the law of death. Satan, deceived by the human nature of Christ, abused his legal power by bringing about His death, and hence ultimately lost dominion over the souls he held captive in hell. Central to this legend is the concept of man as an entirely passive spectator, or non-participant, in the grandiose cosmic struggle between God and the Devil, which enabled his redemption. The Harowing of Hell theme is based on the apocryphal, hence suspect, book of Nicodemus which was rejected as uncanonical in the Dominican *Legenda Aurea* (translated under the title *The Golden Legend of Jacobus De Voragine* by G. Ryan and H. Ripperger, New York, 1941, I, 221) and rejected later in England by both Wyclif and Pecock (H. B. Workman, *John Wyclif*, Oxford, 1926, II, 150; Michael Hurley, S.J., "'Scriptura sola': Wyclif and His Critics," *Traditio*, XVI, 1960, 275-352; Pecock, *Book of Faith*. II. v, cited in J. N. D. Kelley, *Early Christian Creeds*, London, 1950, p. 5).

39. Giovanni Miegge, *The Virgin Mary*, trans. Waldo Smith (Philadelphia, c 1956), a Waldensian attack on Roman Catholic Marian doctrine, insists that the doctrine of co-redemptress has no Gospel authority, and hence constitutes serious error.

40. F. J. E. Raby, *A History of Christian-Latin Poetry* (Oxford, 1927), p. 451. For an account of the numerous legends of the Marian Cult see J. A. MacCulloch, *Medieval Faith & Fable* (Boston, c 1932), chap. vii. One of the most complete and detailed summaries is the *Liber de laudibus gloriosissime dei genetricis Marie* of Albertus Magnus, handsomely printed at Cologne by Ulrich Zell (c 1473; Stillwell A-243; BMC i.192).

41. Émile Mâle, *Art from the Twelfth to the Eighteenth Centuries* (New York, 1949), p. 89; Droulers notes: "St. Michel au moyen âge est toujours représenté dans les scènes du Jugement Dernier avec une balance où il pèse les âmes; et le diable ordinairement est près de là pour faire valoir les intérêts de l'enfer qui réclame sa proie, ou même pour tricher sur la pesée s'il est possible" (*Dict. des attributs, allégories, emblèmes et symboles*, Tournhout, c 1948, s.v. "St. Michel"). Cf. the ME *Tretyse of Loue*: "Loue shall be put in the balaunce of saynt mighel, and that most hath loued shall be glorifyed in heuene" (*EETS OS* No. 223, 1951), p. 4/8-10.

42. Rock (*op. cit.*, III, 160); some 690 churches in England have been dedicated to St. Michael (R. L. P. Milburn, *Saints & Their Emblems in English Churches*, Oxford, 1957), p. 184; other instances of St. Michael and the scales are noted by J. R. Allen, *Early Christian Symbolism in Great Britain and Ireland* (London, 1887), pp. 179-81; Francis Bond, *Dedications of English Churches* (Oxford, 1914), p. 324. Again, this tradition represents man in a passive, spectator role, where more powerful agencies are working on his behalf.

43. *Legenda Aurea*, II. 460-61, sub "The Assumption of the Virgin Mary."

44. See Hope Traver, *The Four Daughters of God* (Bryn Mawr, 1907); Curt F. Bühler (*op. cit.*), pp. 18-37; Samuel C. Chew, *The Virtues Reconciled* (Toronto, 1947), provides 18 plates illustrating this allegory in medieval and Renaissance art; Ralph A. Klinefelter, in *JEGP*, LII (1953), 90-95. Miss Traver's essay, "The Four Daughters of God: A Mirror of Changing Doctrine," *PMLA*, XL (1925), 44-92, promises more than it performs.

45. The topic was debated in the schools: one of the "Questiones" of Stephen

Langton, preserved in St. John's College, Cambridge, MS 57, fol. 148ʳ, reads: "An Deus ex misericordia vel iustitia remuneret. Item utraque istarum vera est." The topic divided the mind of St. Paul himself, if we try to extract consistent theology from his Epistles and do not regard them as merely pastoral: contrast Romans xiv, 10 (or II Corinthians v, 10): "Omnes enim stabimus ante tribunal Christi," with Romans iii, 23-24: "Omnes enim peccaverunt et egent gloria Dei, justificati gratis per gratiam ipsius, per redemptionem quae est in Christo Jesu." Contrasted here is the doctrine of final judgment according to works; and justification, which can only mean divine forgiveness of all previous sins since all men have been unrighteous and hence do not merit salvation. A clear and comprehensive statement of the medieval Church's official position, which harmonizes His Justice and His Mercy, is made by Lawrence V. Ryan, "Doctrine and Dramatic Structure in *Everyman*," *Speculum*, XXXII (1957), 722 ff. Regarding from a different point of view, one might say that the Church was often forced to steer a stormy course between the Scylla of pelagianism and the Charybdis of antinomianism, one medieval form of which might be offered by the recluse who felt that he was in a state of impeccability as a result of having achieved perfected empathy with Christ. A typical warning against such a feeling is voiced by Walter Hilton (*Scale of Perfection*, ed. Dom G. Sitwell, London, 1953), I. xlv: "though this is the truth about the everlasting mercy of God to you and me and all men, we should not therefore, relying on this, be deliberately reckless in our lives." A related debate topic in the schools proves the persistence of the problem: "Quaestio est an creatura per graciam possit fieri inpeccabilis" (cited from Assisi MS 158 by A. G. Little & F. Pelster, *Oxford Theology and Theologians*, c A.D. 1282-1302, Oxford 1934, p. 127).

46. This consolation was often expressed in the concept of the "blissful Passion," or "joy in the Cross" (e.g., Thomas à Kempis, *Imitatio Christi*, II, vi, EETS ES No. 62, 1893, p. 46). Father Harold C. Gardiner has called for the type of modern historical critic who can "feel how essentially right a man of the Middle Ages was when he spoke of the *Blissful* Passion" (*Mysteries' End: An Investigation of the Last Days of the Medieval Religious Stage*, New Haven, 1946, p. xi). Gardiner's view reflects the wholly understandable inclination on the part of some modern Catholic medievalists to chide Protestant medievalists for an alleged lack of sympathetic understanding of the religious life of the Middle Ages (e.g., J. M. Campbell, "Patristic Studies and the Literature of Medieval England," *Speculum*, VIII, 1933, 465-78), and no doubt the voluminous writings of such an obviously biased historian as the late G. G. Coulton would serve as ample justification. There is probably a good deal of truth in what Gardiner says: the concept of the Blissful Passion may be harder to grasp than the more intellectual paradox of the "felix culpa" (see Arthur O. Lovejoy, "Milton and the Paradox of the Fortunate Fall," *ELH*, IV, 1937, 161-79), explicated by Gregory as follows: "Et quidem nisi Adam peccaret, Redemptorem nostrum carnem suscipere nostram non oporteret" (*PL*, LXXIX, 222); or the "felix temptacio" of William of Pagula (*Oculus Sacerdotis*, New College, Oxford, MS 292, fol. 63ʳ): "O felix temptacio, que ad divinos amplexus fugere nos compellit"; or the paradox in the forgiveness speech of Jesus to the contrite Peter, prostrate for shame at his Denial of Our Lord, in the *Chester* Pageant No. xviii (*EETS ES* No. 105, 1916, p. 351, *ll.* 520-24): "Therefore I suffered thee to fall, / that to thy Subiects [the future sinning parishioners of the Church], hereafter, all / that to thee shall cry and call, / thou may have minning. / Sithen thy self so fallen hase, / the more inclyne to graunt Grace!" Orthodox paradoxes are discussed by Rosalie L. Colie, "Time and Eternity: Paradox and Structure in *Paradise Lost*," *Journal of the Warburg & Courtauld Institute*, XXIII (1960), 127-38.

# 2. THE POEMS

## POEM 1

Here begynnes a newe lessoun
Off Crystys ressurrectoun

All this before Ihesu tham sayde
Or handys on Hym thai layde,
That men Hym suld bete & swyng
& on the rode to dede Hym bryng
5  And do schame on all wyse,
And on the thyrd day He wolde ryse.
That tyme was Sabotte in ther lay
That now wyt us es Pasche day.
On that Sabot in the mornyng
10  Wen the day began to spryng
The Magdalene Mary
And othere in hyre company
At the sepulcre redy were,
And oynments with tham ber
15  To smere the body of suete Ihesu
With oynements gode & new.
Als thai stode ther allone
Thus gate makand ther mone,
"Wo sall us helpe the stone to hent
20  Fro the dore of the monument?"
And als thai lyft uppe ther hee
The stone ouer went, thai than see;
Thai lokyd in with outyn othe
& saw nat bot a whyte clothe.
25  Wonder thai had & grete dowte
How the body was brogh with owte.
Bot the Mares nerer thai yede:
Thai fonde angelles in whyte wede
Wyt sterne loke syttand on the stone,
30  That to tham sayd sone onone,

19

"Wemen ye bene in dowte —
Wele I wote ye be abowte
Ihesu to seke of Nazarene
That nayled for yow on rode has ben.
35 He es uppe resyn & not here
Ther thai Hym layde the stede es here.
Ta ye now faithe that ye ne dwelle
To Hys dyssypulles for to telle

(col. 2)

And to Petyr, that He sall be
40 Befor yow all in Galyle.
Ther ye sall se Hym now
Als He befor sayd to yow;
Therfor be ye not in drede,
Seke Hym not emang the dede."
45 The Maryes in ther hartes layde
That Ihesu before to tham sayde
Wyles that He was on lyfve,
And to Hys dyssypulles yed belyve.
The Magdalene scho yede onone
50 And sayd to Peter & to Jone,
"Of the sepulcre My Lord es nomme
And I wote not were He es becomme!"
¶ The Magdalene agayne scho yede
Sayt Peter & Jone to take hede
55 If thai myght on any manere
Of Ihesu outhere se or here.
& forthe scho yede with grete mornyng
Of Ihesu to se summe tokynyng.
As scho wepe & wrang hyre hand
60 Scho saw Ihesu befor hyre stand.
Scho hyre turned & yede ner
& wend it had bene a gardynere.
Than spak Ihesu wyt mylde chere
& hyre askyd on this maner,
65 "Woman for wham wepys thow?
What is thi wylle, wat sekys thow?"
Scho sayd, "My Lord, I af forlorne
That away is hene borne.
If thu Hym hene bar," scho sayd,

20

70   "Telle me wer thu has Hym layd
     & I sall, if it be thi wylle
     Hym thene bere & ga full stylle."
     Be name Ihesu gan Mary newen
     And scho Hym knewe by Hys hewen
75   And to Hys fete scho felle done
     Als scho was wonte for to done.
                           (fol. 153$^r$, col. 1)

     Ihesu bad hyre than forthe wende
     And toche Hym not wyt hyre hende,
     "Bot go to my dyssyples belywe
80   & telle tham I am on lywe
     & that thai sall Me see
     Sone hireaftyre in Galale."
     Synful man here may thu lere
     Of synful woman that was dere,
85   How sothefast luf gan hyre lede
     Ihesu to folo for hyre mede.
     Thus was Mary benedict in synne
     When sewen devles were hyre inne,
     Bot luf hyre dyd mercy wynne
90   Of wylk scho myght never blynne.
     Swete levedy Mary, thi nore,
     We af synned, we wyll no more!
     Thu be for us Hys luf to wyn
     Of Ihesu that the caste oute of syn.
95   For us synful thu be the forespeche
     That He on us tak no wreche.
     That lykyd welle Marie than
     That Ihesu was sywas lywand man,
     And to Hys dyscypulles yede belywe
100   & sayd, "I saw My Lord on lywe
      & sayd thise wordes to me:
      He sall yow se in Galale."
      That dai that Ihesu rose fro dede to lywe
      He schewed Hym sythis fywe
105   Fyrst to Marie that lefte wepyng
      Or scho saw of Hym tokynnyng.
      And ofte to hyr & other mo
      Als He sulde to the cite go.

The thyrd tyme me thynke ryght
110 That Peter had of Hym a syght,
Wen he was allone wente
Hym to seke at the monument.
Wyt two dysypulles at the ferthe tyde
Toward Emaus He yede bysyde
115 And of Holy Writte tham tolde
And thai Hym wold all nyght af holde.

(col. 2)

The tone of tham hyght Cleophas
& the tother hyght Lucas.
That ilk day was so byfall
120 That at even the postylles all
Were in close for the Jues doute
Bot Tomas of Ynde was wyt oute.
In halle thai sate in grate longyng
Of Ihesu to se summe tokynyng
125 & than emong tham gun thai strywe
If He myghte be rysyn to lywe.
Emydes tham tha[n] thai saw Hym stand
& schewed tham bothe fete & hand.
Adred thai ware of that syght
130 For yit thai wenyd not all aryght.
W[o]nder thai had & grete care,
¶ Thai wened a gast had stand thare.
For wen it was & sumdale late,
& sperred were bothe dore & yate,
135 He sayd, "Pes emang yow be,
It es I, ye may me se!
Grapes me fote & hande
That ye may the sothe understande!
Grapes wele, for gast it is none
140 That on hym has flesche & bone,
Als ye may now here se
In hand & fote & syde of Me."
Wen thai were sekyre of this dede
Bothe thai lefte soro & drede;
145 Ioy thai made wyt all ther myght
Wen thai of Ihesu had that syght.
Mo tokyns He schewed tham yette

22

Als sothefast man with tham He ete,
& bad tham overall to preche
150 Hys awne worde the folk to teche;
& so He lefte tham thore styll
& yede ther it was Hys wyll.
Wan He was fro tham gone
Thomas of Inde comme onone;
155 Thai askyd hym, "Were hast thu bene?
We af Oure Lorde sene!"

(fol. 153ᵛ, col. 1)

Thomas ansuerd & sayd, "Nay —
For that noth I lewe may
Bot if I Hys wondys fond
160 & in Hys syd putt my hond.
I lewe it in no wyse
That He myght fro dede ryse."
The sexte day as hit befelle
That Tomas was with the postelles alle
165 & Ihesu stode tham emyde
& to Tomas He sayd, "Abyde —
Tomas thi fyngerys put now here
& in a qwyle thu may lere
In hand, in fote ther the nayles stode
170 The wele I hang on the rode.
In to my syde thi hand now reche
& of my wondys af now knawlege.
That I for the soford sore
In mysbeleve be thu no more."
175 Tomas ansuerd wyt drere chere
"My God, My Lord, Thu hert here!"
Ihesu hym sayd, "For thu me se,
Tomas, wyt thi fleschely hee;
Thu it lewes wele for-thi.
180 Bot thai be blyssyd & celi
That of me saw reght noght
& lewes it wele wyt stedfast toght."
To Hys dyssuples in many wyse
Ihesu Hym chewed fele sythes
185 In water & land, be day & nyght
Ofte the reght belewe to af in syght

23

Bot alle to telle it es no nede
That we of Hym syng & rede.
Gude it es now to say
190 How He ordand us the way
Wen He to Hys Fader wente,
That Hym in to herth sente.
The way He made wen He up yede —
For wyte wele & not it drede
195 That before was never none,
Abrahm, Ysaac, no Saynd Jone,

(col. 2)

That heven myght entyre with inne
Ar that Hym self comme ther inne.
Wen the day comme that Ihesu wolde
200 To heven He styed as He colde.
Wyt Hys dyssypuls fyrst spak & ete,
And sene to the Mownt of Olyvete
Tham led & gaf Hys blyssyng.
& uppe He stye withoutyn dwellyng
205 A lyght clowde Hym bare uppe ryght,
Thro angulls servys & ther lyght.
& als thai stode lokan on hee
Two angels stode tham nee
In mans forme in wyte wede,
210 Tham to comforte & bryng oute of drede,
And sayde, "Ye men of Galele
Standdand — wat behalde ye?
Ihesu that es from yow nome
On that wyse He sall agayne comme.
215 Comme agayn He sall also,
Als ye se Hym to heven go,
At domys day in Hys manhed
To deme bothe qwyk & dede."
Wen Ihesu was oute of ther syght
220 Of the postells left ther no wyght,
Bot ilkon yede to hys stede
As Ihesu had tham before bede
Of the Holy Gost to abyd the sonde
As Ihesu tham dyd understande,
225 There tham in herthe He lete

24

Wen He with tham last spake & ete.
¶ Opon a day was efte befalle
That the postylles alle
In to a howse were commen ilkon
230 Peter, Andrew, James & Jone,
Philipp, Jacob, Tomas, Matheu,
Symon, Jude, Bartylmew,
And other, a fayre company;
Ther thai byd Mayden Mary.
235 Than with lot and holy bede
Thai toke another in Judas stede

(fol. 154r, col. 1)

A postel ches Mathie onone
And of the twelve he made hym one.
Wen the dayes were gone ten sythes fywe
240 Fro that Ihesu ros from dede to lywe,
Hys dyssypulls in that ilk stonde
In that stede were thai fonde,
That oute of heven a dyn thai hard
As a grete wynd temand it fard
245 And the howse fulfylled of hete,
Thare all the postelles in sete;
And sere tonhges ther were sene
That full fere were betwene
That opon tham alle it lyght,
250 The Holy Gost throw Godes myght.
Of the Holy Gost thai ware fild onone
& wyt sere tonges spake ilkone.
Also the Holy Gost tham kened,
That the Fader of heven to tham sened.
255 In [Jerusalem] men myght fynd
That tyme Jues of many kynd
That was betwene erthe & heven
Than thai hard that ilke steve[n].
Wonder thai toght wat it mote bene,
260 And thus thai sayd tham betwene:
"It es not, brethere, als we wene
That we here, wat may this mene?
Brethern, wat say now ye?
Now be this men of Galale

25

265 Ilk man may hym selfe here.
    On ilk speche on ilk manere
    Thai spak of God — may ye not here?"
    Summe sayd that thai drunkynd were
    Than stode Peter up tham betwene,
270 "It es not brethere as we wene
    That this men drunkyn be may
    It es bot undron of the day.
    Now es fulfylled the ald kynd,
    The prophece that God hym send

(col. 2)

275 To oure fadyre & to oure kynd.
    For thus in boke wretyn we fynd
    Oure Lord says it sall befalle
    Opon my servantes alle
    Wen the days draw to hend
280 Of my gost I sall yow send.
    Here prophecie sall be to man here
    The Holy Gost also sal the lere.
    I sall on herthe gyfe tokennys
    & wonder on heght to heven bryng:
285 The son sall wend to myrkenes,
    The mone in blode throgh grete destres,
    Or come the day of God so kene
    In Wham we sall all be sene
    Befor Hym that es heyhe iustis
290 & of Hym dome take after oure servis."
  ¶ Than yede al the postyls for to preche
    The ryght beleve the folke to teche
    The ryght beleve was than ther lore,
    To holde & yong, lasse & more
295 To man & wyfe of alle kynd
    Godes deed to af in mynd.
    & that He up rose & steyed on he
    To Hys Fadyre to sytte Hym nehe,
    On Hys ryght hand wyt Hym to be —
300 O falde God in trinyte!
    Thre Persons in a Godede,
    Wyt Hym to deme bothe quik & dede
    The gode to ioye & wyke to pyne.

No bese ther none, that tham may fyne
305 No sal ther be no motyng
Nor turnay for no gapyng sayng,
Bot ryghtwys dome after thare gylle
Ilke a man to yelde hys whyle
Ioye or pyne take to domede
310 After he al wroght in dede:
Not othyng that he has wroght
Bot the lest thyng that he as thoght
Wyt hert thoght, spokyn with mowthe,
Saynt Austyn says it sall be cowth.

(fol. 154ᵛ, col. 1)

315 In Hys nakyd wysage sal al be sene
And well more than we wene.
No astyre, no syn so stylle efte
Done aganes Goddes wylle
That hym thoght here full lyte
320 That it sal thare hys conscyand byte
For he ne may fynd mercy no grace
No penance to do for hys trespase.
He may no thyng there unleght
So he may unloke hys heght;
325 Of al hys lyf he sal yeld acownte
Wat hys whyt & hys gode amownte.
Demed he bes that ilke stownde
Swelk as hes ther fownde.
Saynt Austyn sayd, "Halo way!
330 What sall I do that ilke day!
On ilke alfe than es my soro,
It es no man that me may boro."
Mi synnes sall myself wray
As I ware worth for to day
335 In the to alf thai sall schew —
My gode dedys that are ful few.
Under me es helle, foule & lothe
O bowe me my domes-man so wrothe;
Myne inwytte mys-lycande,
340 The werld aboute me afyre turnande.
The reght wys sons sall saved be
The synful men — weder may thai fle?

27

Unmyght it es Hym to hyde
& sterne it is that dome to byde,
345   & byde he most on all wyse
For to here peght iustyse,
To take the dome that sal befalle
To hym & to the synful alle.
Of the domes men sal wele here
350   To us say on this manere:
Hym ther it most [halfe] drede
That may hym noder drynk nor fede,
That gaf me no drynk no wold me fede.
Seke, I was, ye wolde me not se;
355   In prison I was, ye comme not to me;

(col. 2)

Nakyd I was, ye gaf me no clothyng;
No ye me wold to howse bryng.
Thai sal answere wyt dref chere
As in the Gospell ye may here,
360   Lorde, qwene saw we The
Seke or in prison be
Hungor hewe, thryst or nede,
Qwen we the warne for to fede;
Nakyd or in any sore
365   & we the warnd al herbore.
Than salle ansuere the reghtwys iustys
And say to tham on this wyse,
That ye dyd sekyre be
To any of myne ye dyd to Me.
370   Than sall thai here the dredfull speche
Wen God of tham sall tak wreche,
Ye cursed gastes hens ye wende
Into that fyre that as none hende;
Thu to be in sore a pyne
375   In helle fyre fro me & myne,
Of the develle to take youre mede
After that ye af worchen in dede —
No bes ther none that than may fle.
The devel wyl al redy be
380   Tham to bere to domunge, & draw
To helle pyne wyt dome & law.

28

Sekyr ye be ther es no kyng, no erel,
Baron, knyht fre, no cherel,
Alde nor yong, pore no ryche,
385 That than may god be swyche,
Nor ersebyschop, prest nor clarke none.
That dome thai sall tak after onone
Alle that oute of this warlde sal wend
Thro fylthe of syn at ther lyves end.
390 Bot thai of that dome sal af no drede
That here thare lyffe with lyght lede,
And here es wythinne tham
No foule spotts of dedeli syn.
For of God ye sall here
395 To tham say on this manere,
"My blyssid chyldyre comes now
Into the blys es made for yow!

(fol. 155ʳ, col. 1)

Hunger I had & ye me fedde,
Nakyd I was & ye me clade,
400 In prison I lay seke & in sore
& ye me gaf harbare —
That ye dyd sekyre ye be
To any of myne ye dyd to me."
Than sall the saules wend to blys
405 As Gods aungels sall, y wys;
In ioye & blys witoutyn pyne,
Als bryght as sone thai sal schyne
In luffe & pes & mekenes,
Ihesu to se in Hys lyknes.
410 Here mai thu, man, se in dede
After the lyf qwat es thi mede.
Thu mai helle or heven chese
Wylk thu wyll holde & qwylk lese.
Yf thu wylt heven wyne
415 The be-hoves to leve syne,
Pryde & wrethe & glotony,
Covetys & envy,
Lychary in all wyse,
Of slawnes in Godys serwyse.
420 This ore the dedly synnys seven.

29

That ledys man way fro heven.
Pryde bryngh man to vnbuxumnes
To grete hart, tyll unmekenes;
Wrath makys man to af sore hond
425 Glotony flemes man oute of lond,
Covetys mas man the devuels fere,
Envyus es lother any gode to here,
Lychory es the devuels oryuall,
In hys baudon he es bonden all;
430 God to serwe slewthe in dede
Gode dedis to do he may not spede.
It es no man that es fownde
In any of thise that ilk stounde
Wan he es of this warlde went,
435 Than he sal to helle withountyn end.
Bot it be the man befall
That af done this syns all
In wyl & thogh[t], in worde & dede,
Ne fall he not in wanhope for no dred

(col. 2)

440 That he ne may marcy wynne
Wyt soro of hart for hys synne.
We rede as Saynt Bernarde saydyn,
Marye es modere & madyn that
For us to byd wyll scho not lette
445 & schues hyre Sone hyre brest swette.
The Sone schewes Hys Fader the syde
Hys blody body, His wondys wyde;
Of mercy may be there no warnyng
Thes es of luf so fayr [tokynyng].
450 My swete frendes take here to hete
Of Mary that es madyn meke:
Hyre brest undose hyre Sone to qwame
Fro helle pyne us to yeme.
Thyng also on the woundes
455 That Ihesu tholede for the in stoundes
And es abowte in pese to wyn
That thu as lost thro gylte of syn.
Th[r]o Hys Fader He is sure forespeche
That He on us take no wreche.

30

460 Yf He be siddele wroth i founde
     Us to chastys & mende af munde
     He sall wende agayne efte sone
     For Hys serwantes to get ther bone.
   ¶ My leve frendes that this boke herrs,
465 Graunte me this in ȝoure prayers:
     For us to byd to Ihesu mylde
     Forin ys mercy that He us schelde
     Fro wyckyd wyl, syn & schame,
     That we no drof of Hym no blame.
470 And if I do any gode dede
     I graunt yow all part to mede —
     Reght it es ilkon for othere
     Byd to God as sylk for brother.
     And He that us to lyve broght
475 Wen He us on the rode boght,
     Wyt Hys blode He gyf us grace
     In Hys ryche to se Hys face,
     On Hym to loke, on Hym to se
     In ioye & blys with Hym to be.
480 Of that blys may no man tell
     How grete it es may no man spell
     Ne hart thynk nor hee se,
     Nor here here qwylk it sal be.

     Ther es plente withouten nede
485 Sekyrnes wythoutyn drede,
     Evell to do es ther no myght,
     Ther es day wytoutyn nyght,
     Wytoutyn sore, wytoutyn care
     All that es gode men sall af thare.
490 To that blys Ihesu us bryng
     That to Hys Fader made offeryng
     Wyth His flesche & with Hys blode
     There hang opone the rode.
     That es gode & aye sall be
495 With the Holy Gost in Trinite.
     Thedere mot we all wende!
     And thare to be withouten ende!
     And ever ilk man forthy

(fol. 155ᵛ, col. 1)

A Pater Noster & a Ave Mary
500   That Ihesu ofte us grace sende
Wyt Hym to won withoutyn ende!

Explicit

## POEM 2

Also take hede to this insawmpyl here
That is lykend vnto the fawconere,
The whilk when his hawke fro hym dos flee
Schews to the hawke rede flesche to see;
5   And when the hawke lokes ther vnto
Fast to his mayster he hastes to go.
Thus do on Criste as ꝫe may see
Hynges bledyng opon a tree,
Hys body with blody woundes schewynge
10   For to reduce to Hym mans saule & brynge
The whilk fro Hym by syn dos fle away,
And to Hym wilt turne agayn with outen delay.
Thus He has tew armes spred, man to hald & kysse
That to Hym by luf wil turne repentyng his mys.
15   Therfore of salvacoun if thu sure wil be
The cros of penaunce thou take on the:
That is be discret poneschyng of thi body,
And nayled thorow thi left hande for thi foly
With schame & displesaure of all thi syn
20   Thatt letts the alway heuen to wyn.
The nayle in the right hande also sal be
Desyre & luf of heuenly thinges in thi hert fre;
The nayle sal be dred that thorw thi fete sal go
That in dedly syn thu be not dampned to endles wo,

ED. NOTE: Lines 1-2 are written in red ink. On l. 9 a "wt" has been dotted for erasure after "blody." On l. 23 "hert sal go" has been dotted for erasure before "fete sal go."

32

25 And the spere the whilk sal perche thi hert
  Sal be contricoun for syn with sorow smert.
  The blode & the watyr that fro the hert ryns clere
  Sal be wepyng for the syns thu has done here,
  Thus thi self here thou sal do crucifye
30 That aftyr in blis thu may be set full hye.

## POEM 3

(fol. 179ᵛ)

This es the byginnyng hwich cristenman owe for to hafe a remembraunce of the passioun of our lord Jesu Criste.

  Of alle the ioyus that in this worlde may be
  That thorw wyt to man myth be ordeyned & wroute,
  A swete lofe thowt is praised of me
  For alle other ioyus i-sette at nowte.
5 For wen the thowtus of the herte ben in heuen aboue,
  And ther thoru grace ben holde full stylle,
  And in the trinite is loke fast thi loue,
  And the terus ren down be thi lerus so stylle
  And thow thenkust on that derne loue so swete,
10 That thi Lorde hath loued the so longe by fore
  And sorus the of thi synnes so grete
  And in wylle to louen hem no more,
  Then ioyus thi soule thoru Goddys mythe
  And hoputh that welthus for hure is wrohte
15 And scyneth ful clere befor Goddys syhte,
  Then is he in loue longynge y-browte,
  And in stylle mornyng he halt hure stylle
  And desyruth owt of this world be browte

(fol. 180ʳ)

  There he myhte euer fulful Goddes wylle,
20 And loue Hym and serue Hym & neuer gylt Hym nowte.
  Me thenketh in no ioyus that in this world may be,
  Myhte man neuer wyselokur begynne
  Than swete loue thowtes i-sette in the trinite
  Heuen to perse & ther hore wonnyng to wynne.

              33

25 Of alle the vertuus that in man may be
It neynt nexte the heye godhede.
A swete loue thowt in charite
It feduth & norycheth alle gostlych dede.
Man als ofte as the is ʒeue sweche grace
30 Suche swete loue thowtes wyth the to be,
Bisy the to holdun hem in that place
And hery fast that God that sent hem the,
For of thi self ne commuth ther nowte
Bot of ʒefte thoru grace of the holy goste
35 Wyche is bysy to putte in vs that swete loue thowte,
And euer more in erthe is oure comford moste.
And euer He bisuth Hym be day & be nyhte
Oure loue thowtes to drawen an hey,
And ther to leren thoru grace a-ryhte
40 Wat dwellyng in ioye God hath dyhte hym ney.
To alle tho that here wyth wylle and thowte
Trowely wylle louen Hym & of Hym hafe drede
That ioyful duellyng for hem God hath wrowte
In that endles blysse to qwyte her mede.
45 Man hafe thi kynde Lord oft in thi thowte,
And thenke how myche He coueytuth the loue of the
For alle the gode that He hath for the wrowte
He desyruth not but thi lowe in charite.
A loue thowte myn herte hath wonded sore
50 To morne oft I may fynd wy,
Of sorus to fele sculd I neuer more
If I were kynd and bethowte me redyly

(fol. 180ᵛ)

For wen I be thenke me I wysse
On Hym that alle my loue is on
55 He ioynt me no worldly blysse,
For seyʒtus that I see Hym upon.
ʒif I be hold fram top to too
Seyʒtus of sorue I may see thore:
Hys swete body was wrappid alle in wo,
60 Wyth blode & bytter wondus sore.
ʒif I byholde on Hys blyssed heued
That gouernuth both heuen & helle,
Wyth a wrethe of thornes I see it be weued;

34

The thornes thrullud that blyssud felle
65 Euery thorne had made a wonde.
I see Hym blede & smert ful sore
That syhte wyth sorue myn herte hath bonde
For dulful paynes that I see thore.
ʒif I byholde on Hys face so schene
70 Wyth blodi stremus alle ouer was runne,
May no man in herte deme
The soruus that to Hym were by gonne.
Hys blyssed mouthe that was so swete
Wyth a cos of tresoun so was He mete,
75 Wyth galle and eyselle Hys thrust to lete
Opon a sponge to Hys mouthe was sette.
Alle these peynes bytere and sore
My dere Lord tholede with moche woo;
ʒif y be-holde forthere more
80 I may fynde wel many moo.
I see my Lord with wrathe & onde
I-strept al naked was He tho,
I-bounde bothe fet and honde
To a piler with moche wo.
85 With scharpe skourges He was y-bete —
That blissful body ther He stod,

(fol. 181ʳ)

The strokes maden wondes grete
Wel faste they ronnen on rede blod;
His body that was so whyʒt as flour
90 Tender & softe & of a maden y-bore,
Ther was He torned to a red colour
Ther skourget, y-wonded, & al to-tore.
Nine thousand woundes bytere & sore
His body swete soffrede tho,
95 So fele rede stremes rennyng by-fore
Was neuer er seyen in no wo.
I se that lomb with outen lac
So mekliche toward Hys deth go,
Bering the holy croys on His bac
100 With bitere peynes & muche wo.
With blod & water He was be-swat
To wayʒschen vs wrecches out of oure wo;

35

For mannes loue He soffrede al that
To wreken vs of oure dedliche fo.
105 Ther was seytes of sorwe y-founde
Who so wole ther to take good kepe;
Lytil loue may in his herte be founde
That wol nau3t for that si3t wepe.
With a cloth of purpel He was be weued,
110 In despit of my dere Lord tho,
To the fley3s[h] wyth the blod faste hit cleued.
Tho bygan to Hym a newe wo:
Whenne the cloth was clongen His body two
And the blod was coled there vp on
115 His enemyes with ful muche wo
Redliche they breden hit fram His bodi anon;
Many a pece of His fley3s was tore
His swete body was al to-rent.
So my3ty a kyng was neuer byfore

(fol. 181ᵛ)

120 On erthe y-sene so foule y-schent.
His blesside body al bledynge
Was leyd opon a cros of tre;
Who so wole of His peynes haue knowynge
Behold there & 3e may sorwes y-se.
125 His blessede handes were drawen a-twynne
With ropes stronge, with moche woo;
Ar they my3te the holes wynne
Euery ioynt was drawn a two.
They token longe nayles tweyne
130 Thoru3 euery hond they dreuen on:
The blod sprang out of euery ueyne,
The hote blod ouer the colde ron.
Allas why nele man haue in mende
The dolful sy3tes he my3te se thore!
135 Senne hath mad vs wrecches so blinde
We mowe nou3t se His peynes sore.
Whan He was nayled thoru3 both His honde
Wel faste to the harde tre,
With a rop His bledyng legges they bound
140 And drowen on Hym withoten pite.
They halede along His body thoo

36

That alle His veynes gonne to crake;
Euery senwe was borston a-twoo
Er they my3te the thridde hole take.
145 The thridde nayl they token anon
Was row3 & long & somdel gret
They sparedon nethther senwe no bon,
They dreuen Hym thoru3 both His fet.
Tho hadde He foure grisly wondes moo;
150 Faste they ronnen on rede blode.
Euere His peynes were mo & mo,
And al hit was for oure gode.

(fol. 182ʳ)

They rereden on the croys with strengthe
And setten hit on an hel an hey3 —
155 Ther heng my lord on brede & longthe;
Many a man that sorwe sey.
They py3ten hit doun with wraththe & honde
That was to Hym a peyne ful sore.
Mi Lord heng there be fot & honde
160 All His membris to-borsten thore.
Tho was His bed mad on nayles thre
To resten His wery body on;
His pilwe was of thornes, as 3e may se,
His blody heued they cleued hit opon.
165 There was sorwe who so wolde be-holde
Opon Caluarye the gode Fryday,
To sen a kyng that al may wolde
Hangen in so dolful aray.
There was the baner of lyf displayed
170 His standard was py3 on an hey hil.
There bod that kyng in the feld arayed
With blody sydes and woundes gril;
His colours were bothe wanne & rede
Bloke & blody on euery syde;
175 Wolde He nou3t fle for harm & drede
Or He hadde feld the deueles pride.
He abod that dolful batayle there
To fulfulle His Fader wille,
And to geten a3en His tresor dere
180 That the fend hadde wonnen thoru3 his gile.

37

Ther was the delfullest batayle ydon
That euer was seththen this world was wrouth.
That so my3ty a kyng that gilt hadde non
So spitousliche scholde to dethe be brou3th.

185 Witnesse on His moder so dere

(fol. 182ᵛ)

That saw3 al that batayle & al that tene;
Sche lokede on Hym wyth drery chere
Whoche were here sorwes, may no man deme.
Sche was wrapped with inne & oute
190 With sorwe & mournyng and moche wo.
His enemyes were so thycke aboute
Sche my3t nou3t ones comen Hym to.
To deye ry3t there hit was here wille
Whenne sche say her der Sone in al that strif,
195 And the iewes aboute, His fley3sch to spille,
That was here herte, her loue, her ioye, her lyf —
Blody teres sche let doun renne.
Here herte with sorwe wounded was sore,
Cam a time sche swonede thenne,
200 Nas neuer moder so wo for-chid byfore.
Ther heng that blissful lomb of lyf
By twene to theuis al naked tho.
He abod euer mekliche in al that stryf
And tholede al the sorwes that men wolde Hym do.
205 3if y bethenke me wel with inne
Many mo peynes may y there se
That my Lord tholed for man synne
Whan He heng y nayled on the tre.
So strong a cold a-ful that day
210 Was nou3t feled long by-fore.
That kyng heng in dolful aray,
His clothing was rent and al to-tore;
The skyn that His swete fley3sch was wrapped in
Woch He hadde of Hys modir take
215 Many thousand holes were mad therin
With thornes, skourjus, & nayles blake.
The bitternesse of that colde wynd
Asayled His body on euery syde

(fol. 183ʳ)

And hosliche on Hym blew byfore & byhynd
220 And scharpliche a serchid His woundus wyde.
So fele peynis & stormus as He soffred tho
May neuer no man in herte deme.
To saue His schep His wille was tho —
His loue was trewe, hit was wel y-sene:
225 As a god schipherde on hye hullus
He kepte His schep fram woluus wylde;
In wyndus & hayles & wederus
And other stormus that ben nou3t mylde.
Under a thorn He wole hem kepe
230 Til the feble wederus ben comen & gon;
Thane He wole fetten a3en togedre His schepe
And br[i]nge hem into here kende leswe anon.
So dede that blessed herde of loue
Wel stille abod vnder a thorn.
235 On the heye hul of Caluarie aboue
He abod there many a biter storm,
But as sone as the stormes were ouer-schake
He wolde no longur in sorwes endure
But sette His schep that were astrake
240 And brou3te hem a3en to here kende pasture.
Of alle schiperdus y-blessed mot He be
That euer kepte schepe in felde other in toun,
That so freli bou3te His schep a3e
That were so faste in helle prisoun.
245 He lokede on His enemyes alle
That hadde y-wrou3t Hym al that wo;
Swete teres He let doun falle,
For deel they nolde turnen Hym two.
To His Fader ful mekliche He seyde,
250 "In to thyn hond my spirit y be-take."
His heued wel dolfullich a doun He leyde

(fol. 183ᵛ)

And deyde ther for mannus sake.
The[r] 3e may se the moste pite
That euer was in this world y-don —
255 By-thenk wrecche al hit was for the!
His peynes passede martirdom.
Longius brou3te a spere ful kene

39

And sette hit to His swete syde,
Thoru3 biddyng of His enemyes breme.
260 He made there a wounde ful wyde —
His swete herte that was so clene
With that spere was opened tho.
Ther ran out watir & blod ful schene,
That was raunsom of our wo;
265 There was mercy y-seye ful son:
The kny3 hadde y-ben blyn ful longe
The herte blod by the spere doun ron,
He felede hit wet upon his honde
Ther-with he wypede bothe his ey3en.
270 Thoru3 that blod he hadde the grace,
Anon that body ful wel he sey3e
That there was honged in that place.
"Mercy!" he gan crie ful sone,
And in his herte he sikede sore.
275 The Fader of heuene herde his bone,
Hit was for-3euen hym ry3t thore.
So was blynd ful longe to fore,
Mannys soule thoru3 dedli sinne,
Oure sy3t was geten a3en ry3t thore,
280 Thoru3 red blod rennyng & woundes grimme.
Tho was fulfeld the prophesie
That Symeon seyde Oure Lady to,
That the swerd of sorwe ful many a sythe
Thorw3 out here herte scholde go.

(fol. 184ʳ)

285 Whanne He was cold stif and ded
And hadde ouer comen al that wo,
His frendes token him to red
Of the croys to taken Hym tho.
Whanne He was of the croys ytake
290 Toward a graue they gonnen Hym bere,
Ther com His moder in al that wrake
Wepyng with a rewly chere.
Sche bad sche moste here Sone beholde
That the iewes hadde so foule for-fare;
295 Sche fond alle His frendes cold;
After deth wel faste sche willede thare.

40

Tho Marie say here Sone so dere
Al blody of that rode ydon
Ther nas [no] sorwe to schewen there
300 Bytwene here and here cosyn Jon.
No wonder nas that sche wep sore:
Sche saw3 ligge by fore here than
The fley3sch that was of here body bore
Ded and cold and al to-tore and wan.
305 Sche wonede there ful many a sythe;
His colde mouth sche kulte ful swete;
Teres ronnen there ful rine
With sykyng & gronyng & mourny[n]g eke.
Was neuer so dolful a metyng
310 As was by twene hem twene tho,
Ne neuer so rewlich a partyng
Whenne Crist was boran His moder fro.
They token that rewlich body there,
In linnen cloth they wounden Hym anon;
315 In to a graue they Hym bere,
And helede Hym with a lyd of ston.
There lay my Lord in graue ful stille

(fol. 184ᵛ)

With al His woundes mo than fiue.
The thridde day thoru3 His owne wille
320 He ros a3en fram deth to lyue;
To heuene He stey3 thoru3 His my3th
There His dwellyng for euer schal be.
His gloriouse face that is so bry3th
Ihesu graunte vs grace there to se!
325 Dere Lord Thi peynes were stronge Thu tholedest for me!
And euer the lengor they were more & more —
Dere Lord Thy woundes were wyde Thu tholedest for me!
Ful bittere they smorten and oken sore —
Dere Lord Thy blod was ful red Thu tholedest for me!
330 Hit ran ryue on euery syde —
Dere Lord Thy deth was ful strong Thu tholedest for me!
Many wonderful toknes witnesseth that tyde
Whene y thenke on alle these sorwes ryue
That my dere Lord tholede for loue of me.
335 Allas how scholde y be glad or blyue

41

For ony worldes ioye that y may now se!
He louede vs wel, hit was wel y-sene that stounde
On the Fryday of mercy who so wole by-holde,
Whaune He tholede alle His peynes & wounde
340  On His blissid body with cares colde.
He ȝaf al His fleyȝsch, bones & blod,
Herte & synwis for loue of man,
Water and veynis — His loue was god —
He twynnede His soule His bodi fram.
345  Man in thyn herte thouȝ haue pite,
Thenk on Hym that tholede for the al this peyne
Fram endles deth to bringe the;
And bryngge the to thy ryȝth heritage & reyne.
To quite The, Lord, haue y no myȝt —
350  Thy loue that was to me so strong;

(fol. 185ʳ)

Whenne y thenke on alle Thy peynes ariȝt,
ȝif y loue sinne thenne do y wrong.
Thre borwys, Lord, y schall The fynde,
Thi wille thoruȝ grace of The to folfulle
355  To amende the fautes that hath be by-hynde
That y haue so moche wrout aȝens Thy wille.
My loue schal, Lord, to The so be loke
That hit schal neuer by taken The fro;
Thy peynes scholle, Lord, in myn herte so be stoke
360  That they scholle neuere fram me go.
Redlich sinne, Lord, y schal for Thy loue forsake
That y wolle neuere louen hem na mo;
In to Thy mercy, Lord, y me be-take
Body and soule, in wele and wo.
365  Thy peynes, Thy woundes, Thy blod so red,
Thy deth that was to The so strong —
I clepe The to helpe aȝens the qued
Whanne y schal wexen bothe def & domb.
To Thy mercy, Lord, thanne moche nedeth me
370  For other help thanne haue y non,
Bote Thi peynes & deth Thu tholedest for me
To kepe me fram my grislych fon.
Be ryȝt of rest to asken The
I am vnworthy to ben so bold,

375 My werkes han be so unwyse to The,
    In al my lyue bothe ʒong and old.
    Bote Thy loue maketh me ful hardy to be
    In Thy mercy to leue and triste,
    Withouten ende Thy seruaunt to be
380 In wele and wo, in peyne and reste —
    Al myʒty God in trinite —
    For alle Thy passiouns st[r]ong & ryue
    That Thouʒ tholedest with moche humylite,

                                    (fol. 185ᵛ)

    On gode Friday twenty and fyue.
385 Haue mercy on me at my deth daye
    And sende me grace so to serue The,
    That y may come to that endles ioye
    To se The, my God, in trinite.
    Als wis, Lord, as Thu haddest mercy & mynde
390 On that thef that heng by The,
    Whenne Thu so dere bouʒtest mankynde
    On gode Friday on the harde tre.
    Als wis, Lord, haue mercy on me at myn endyng
    And fram the foule fend schilde Thowʒ me,
395 Whane my body & soule schal twynne
    Lat hym on my soule haue no pouste.
    But dere Lord, thorwʒ Thy passioun graunte me to wynne
    The blisse that euer more schal be;
    At my deth for-ʒeue me my sinne,
400 Ich by-seche The my Lord in trinite!

# 3. NOTES TO THE POEMS

## POEM 1

*Title* ] lessoun (cf. cognates: "lecture," "legend"). The liturgical and homiletic "lectio" led to public prayer, the "lectio" of the schools led to the "questio" and "disputatio"; the "divina lectio" of the cenobitic or eremitic life led to the "meditatio"; and "oratio" (cf. the Carthusian *Scala Claustralium*, PL, CLXXXIV, 476: "Oratio est devota cordis intentio in Deum pro malis amovendis et bonis adiscendis"): the object and method of the second is science and reason, the object and method of the third is wisdom and faith. Anselm's famous "credo ut intelligam" attempts to harmonize the two attitudes, but the whole history of medieval thought argues that the conflict was insoluble. At the level of the laity the conflict was no doubt grasped in a manner similar to that shown in the following ME verses:

> Wytte hath wondyr that Reson tell ne can,
> Houh a mayde bare a chylde both god & man;
> Therfor leve wytte & take to the wundyr —
> Feyth goth a-bove, & Reson goth vndyr.

(Carleton Brown, *Religious Lyrics of the XVth Century*, Oxford, 1939, No. 119.) The schoolmaster would argue that Scripture cannot be understood without being chewed and digested by disputation: e.g., Peter the Chanter, *Verbum Abbreviatum* (PL, CCV, 13): "In tribus igitur consistit exercitum sacrae Scripturae: circa lectionem, disputationem et praedicationem.... Disputatio quaesi paries est in hoc exercitio et aedificio: quia nihil plene intelligitur, fideliterve praedicitur, nisi prius dente disputationis frangatur." The eremite would argue that: "non disputando sed amando scietur" (Richard Rolle, *Incendium Amoris*, ed. M. Deanesley, Manchester, 1915, p. 41). St. Bernard in his assault on the alleged "rationalism" of Abelard charged that: "Petrus Abaelardus christianae fidei meritum evacuare nititur dum totum quod Deus est, humana ratione arbitratur se posse comprehendere" (*Epist.*, No. cxci, PL, CLXXXII, 357). It is worth noting that in England, after the 1382 censure of Wyclif and the consequent end of carefree academic debate, the term "heresy" was often equated with "rationalism," with the alleged ele-

44

vation of human reason above the authority of revelation; e.g., Thomas Gascoigne, the bitter opponent of Reginald Pecock, in his *Loci e Libro Veritatum*, ed. Thorold Rogers (Oxford, 1881), p. 117, s.v. "haereticus."

*1-6* The poem starts so abruptly that it may be regarded as being acephalous.

*3* swyng ] buffet, beat.

*7* lay ] belief, creed.

*12* And othere. Cf. *Southern Passion* (EETS OS No. 169, 1927), *ll.* 1697-98: "Marie Magdaleyn and Marie Iacobee / Oure lady sister and another ek, Marie Salomee." In the *Ludus Coventriae* (EETS ES No. 120, 1922), No. 36, each of the Three Maries introduce themselves in oratorical set-speeches.

*14-44* Follows Mark xvi, 1-7, fairly closely.

*18* gate ] began, started.

*35-44* Follows Luke xxiv, 4-8.

*37* dwelle ] delay.

*48* belyve ] quickly, at once.

*58* tokynyng ] sign, manifestation; a favorite term in ME devotional writing.

*60-82* Follows John xx, 11-17.

*62* gardynere. Being literal-minded, our author does not indulge in hermeneutic elaboration. The theme of Christ the gardener, the "hortulans qui eradicavit mortem," who planted with lilies the garden of vices represented by the character of Mary Magdalene, was a medieval favorite; cf. Vincent of Beauvais, *Speculum Historiale* (Nuremberg, 1485), IV, i; St. Bernard's sermon on Christ as a spiritual gardener (*PL*, CLXXXV, 212); the ME *Pepysian Gospel Harmony* (EETS OS No. 157), p. 103.

*78* toche Hym not. The reason for this admonition (the famous "noli me tangere"), following John xx, 17, is given in *Ludus Coventriae*, No. 37, *ll.* 42-43 : "Towche me not as ȝett, Mary / Ffor to my fadyr I haue not Ascende"; *Southern Passion*, *ll.* 1892-93: " 'Ne touche me nouȝt,' quath Ihesu, 'ne nothing of my felle, / Ffor y nam nouȝt ȝut ysteye to me ffader, and to ȝoure ffader al-so.' "

*80* lywe = lyfe. The scribe frequently writes *w* for *f*.

*89* luf. ME accounts explain the First Appearance to Mary Magdalene on the basis of her great love ("by cause ho lufd so tenderly," *Stanzaic Life of Christ*, EETS OS No. 166, 1926, *l.* 7552). Furthermore: "that was soo holy a womon, that our Lorde Ihesu Crist aftyr his modyr louyd her most of all woymen . . . that dyde penaunce and repentyng that scho had lost by lust of flesch and sore synnyng" (Myrc, *Festial, EETS ES* No. 96, 1905, p. 203).

*90* blynne ] cease.

*91* nore ] pupil.

*95* forespeche ] pleader.

*98* sywas ] surely.

*104* sythis fywe. Full elaboration of the Five Appearances is accumulated in the *Legenda Aurea* ("De Resurrectione Domini," I, 221 ff.); *Stanzaic Life of Christ, ll.* 7530-7800.

*117-18* The two Peregrini; cf. Luke xxiv, 13. *Towneley* Pageant, No. 27 (*EETS ES* No. 71, 1897) expands this topic.

*121* for the Jues doute = "for fear of the Jews": John xx, 19: "et fores essent clausae ubi erant discipuli congregati propter mutum Judaeorum."

*125* strywe = strive ] discuss, debate.

*127* Emydes ] among.     MS repeats tham.

*131* MS Wnder.

*134* sperred ] locked, fastened: cf. John xx, 19.

*135* John xx, 21.

*137* grapes ] touch.

*154 ff.* The topic of the Doubt of Thomas has been explored recently by Eleanor Prosser (*op. cit.*), pp. 147-78, who notes that none of the accounts in the Gospels agree, and that all of the disciples were to some degree "doubting Thomases" since they all had some mental reservations about the validity of the Resurrection. The doubt of Thomas constituted sin.

*158* noth ] not.

*166-74* John xx, 27; cf. *Early South English Legendary* (*EETS OS* No. 87, 1887), No. 56, *ll*, 13-14: "Ore Louerd seide, 'Thomas, hider thi finguer: and pult here into mi side, / And ne beo nou3t in mis-bi-leue: for mine woundene thou sixt wide.'"

*176* hert = art (the scribe frequently adds an *h* before vowels, as in the hee = eye of *l.* 178 below; and the herth = earth of *l.* 192 below).

*180* celi ] blessed.

*191* Cf. *Towneley* Pageant No. 29, *ll.* 256-57: "hevyn behold and se / how Ihesus vp can weynde."

*196* Cf. William of Nassyngton, *Speculum Vitae* (Lansdowne MS 388, fol. 377r); "Habraham, Isaac, Jacobe & Seint John / That

46

enter heuen ne myght within / Er that hym selue com theder with wynne." According to the Harrowing of Hell tradition based on the apocryphal book of Nicodemus (chap. xx), Christ liberated all sinners, including the patriarchs and the prophets, from the prison of hell and led them to heaven where they found already there Elijah, Enoch, and Dismas (the thief crucified at Calvary next to Jesus). John the Baptist accosted them and obtained their explanations of why they were in heaven (in the *Chester* Pageant No. 17, *EETS ES* No. 105, 1916, *ll.* 213-56, Adam does the accosting).

200 styed ] ascended.

202 sene ] afterward.

*211-12 Actus Apostolorum* i, 10-11: "... Viri Galilaei, quid statis aspicientes in caelum?"

217-18 Allusion to the eschatological topic of Doomsday (see Introduction above, pp. 6-7): for ME accounts of the Last Judgment see *EETS OS* No. 24, 1867, pp. 118-25; *Speculum*, XIX (1944), 421-32; *EETS OS* No. 69, 1878, s.t. "St. Jeremie's 15 Tokens before Doomsday" (analysis by P. Kretzmann, *The Liturgical Element in the Earliest Forms of the Medieval Drama*, Minneapolis, 1916).

223 sonde ] message, visitation.

224 understande ] explain, inform.

225 lete ] lead, guide.

*235-38 Actus Apostolorum* i, 26: "Et dederunt sortes eis, et cecidit super Mathiam" (Judas, in wanhope, had committed suicide).

*241-42 Actus Apostolorum* ii, 2: "erant omnes pariter in eodem loco."

247 sere ] many.

255 MS iehm.

258 steven ] voice.

268 *Actus Apostolorum* ii, 13: "Alii autem irridentes dicebant: Quia musto pleni sunt isti." The Latin word "mustum" was often taken into ME literally as "must" (e.g., *The Wycliffite Bible*, ed. Forshall and Madden, Oxford, 1850), and the detail interested English writers; cf. Bede's characteristic "mystical" comment (*Expositio Actuum Apostolorum*, ed. M. L. W. Laistner, Medieval Academy of America Pub. No. 35, Cambridge, Mass., 1939, p. 17): "Inridentes licet mystice tamen vera testantur, qui non vino veteri quod in nuptiis ecclesiae defecit sed musto sunt gratiae spiritualis impleti. Iam enim vinum novum in utres novos venerat, cum apostoli non in vetustate litterae sed in novitate spiritus dei magnalia resonarent."

*272* undron = the third hour, from nine to twelve in the morning; or 9:00 A.M. Meditations on the Passion are often segmented into different canonical hours (e.g., "Bonaventura," *Privity of the Passion,* in Horstmann, *Yorkshire Writers,* I, 204; William of Shoreham, *Hours of the Cross,* EETS ES No. 86, 1902, pp. 79-85).

*273* kynd ] rightful; the allusion is to the prophecy of Joel (*Actus Apostolorum,* ii, 17).

*276-80* Cf. *Actus Apostolorum* ii, 18: "Et quidem super servos meos, et super ancillas meas, in diebus illis effundam de Spiritu meo, et prophetabunt." The ME *Speculum Sacerdotale (EETS OS* No. 200, 1935), p. 160, speculates that: "afore the tyme of the aduent of the Holy Gost the apostles were so bowynge, flexible, and vnconstant or vnstable that Peter, that was the hede of hem, denyede his lorde and his maister at the voice of an ancylle, *scilicet,* a damsel that was seruant in the place."

*300* falde ] folded (?), hence enclosed, thence manifested.

*304* fyne ] aphetic for refine (purify through contrition, confession, and penance).

*305* motyng ] pleading.

*306* turnay ] attorney. Cf. *Pricke of Conscience* (ed. R. Morris, Berlin, 1863), *ll.* 6083-84: "For-why thai sal than na help gett / Of sergeaunt, ne auturne, ne avoket."

*307* Construe: But righteous judgment according to their guilt.

*308* yelde hys whyle ] accept his sentence, or time; or admit his deceit.

*309* take to domede ] accept as his reward, sentence. MS has a superfluous "me" dotted for erasure before the "mede" of "domede."

*312* Alluding to such venial sins as flattery, coming late to church, etc.; for lists see *Pricke of Conscience, ll.* 3432-3502, s.v. "septies in die cadit iustus"; cf. Chaucer, "Parson's Tale," *l.* 357: "And venial synne is it, if man love Jhesu Crist lasse than hym oghte *(Complete Poetical Works,* ed. F. N. Robinson, p. 238); and subsequent analysis and listing in *ll.* 357-85; Walter Hilton, *Scale of Perfection* (ed. & trans. Dom G. Sitwell, London, 1953), I.xlvi. Cf. the ME *Of Deadly and Venial Sin* (Horstmann, *Yorkshire Writers,* I, 183): "For to assent sodanly is venial synne: bot for to couete or assent be avysment, that is dedly synne."

*314, 329* Quotations from St. Augustine have not been traced; but it is possible that his august name is being invoked to lend the passages authority — a not uncommon phenomenon. I notice that several

48

alleged quotations from Augustine in Chaucer's "Parson's Tale" are likewise untraced (see notes in Robinson's 2nd ed. to *ll.* 368, 383): such matters raise puzzling questions about the transmission and availability of medieval texts.

317 astyre ] disturbance.

321-22 ME Doomsday accounts often fail to make clear that the Last Judgment is properly after the resurrection of Christians ("resureccio mortuorum"); on earth it is never too late to repent of one's sins: the sinner who is unable or unwilling to repent is in a state of despair, or wanhope, and is guilty of a sin against the Holy Ghost (Judas's despair displeased Jesus more than the Betrayal; cf. *Southern Passion, ll.* 1403-4: "Iudas wrathede more oure lord, myd wanhope that he hadde / Than tho he solde him to the dethe"; *Speculum Christiani*, EETS OS No. 182, 1933, p. 206: "Iudas offended god more in that he henge hym-selfe than in that he be-trayede Criste," et cetera), as the ME *Jacob's Well* (EETS OS No. 115, 1900), p. 85, makes clear: "art so full of foly, that thou trustyst noght in the mercy of god; for thou thynkest that god may noght forgeue the thi synne; & so, in that wanhope, thou makyst god mercyles, & in this ouer-hope thou fordoost his ryghtwysnes." Similar statements are in *Handlyng Synne* (EETS OS No. 123, 1903), *ll.* 12297-98; *Book of Vices and Virtues* (EETS OS No. 217, 1943), p. 24; *Middle English Sermons* (EETS OS No. 209, 1940), 57/3-8. *The Pricke of Conscience* seems to me to reflect orthodox dogma as well as proper priestly concern for the sinner; after stating that at the Last Judgment (i.e., after the death of the sinner) he "sal be dampned withouten mercy" yet:

> Na man tharfor suld in dispayre be;
> For alle that has mercy here sal be save,
> And alle that here askes mercy sal it have,
> Yf thai it sekes whilles thai lyf bodily
> And trewely trayste in Goddys mercy,
> And amende tham and thair syn forsake,
> Byfor the tyme ar the dede tham take . . .
> Bot if the dede byfor haf tham tane
> Ar thai haf mercy, than gette thai nane. (*ll.* 6293-6303)

323 unleght ] unlighten, alleviate.

324 unloke hys heght ] mitigate his sentence.

328 hes = he is.

332 boro = borrow ] redeem, ransom.

*333* wray ] accuse, charge.

*335* in the to alf ] on both sides.

*339* myslycande ] distasteful.

*343* unmyght ] impossible.

*346* peght ] pitched, hence determined, passed.

*350-71* Draw heavily on Matthew xxv, 42-46.

*351* MS blurred.

*358* dref chere ] troubled expression.

*360 ff.* (and *ll.* 398-401 below) Cf. the Seven Deeds of Mercy topic, developed in most ME works of pastoral instruction: e.g., *The Vij Bodyly Dedes of Mercy:* "Fede the hungry; Gyf drynke to the thyrsty / Clothe the naked; herber the howsles / Vysett the seeke; Delyuyr prisoners / And bery the pour whan they be deed" (Cambridge Univ. Library MS Hh. 3.13, fol 111ʳ). The standard work on the medieval obsession with numerical tabulation and numerology is by V. F. Hopper, *Medieval Number Symbolism* (New York, 1938).

*362* hewe = heve ] have.

*363* warne ] refuse, deny.

*368-9* sekyre ] assuredly, certainly; the lines render Matthew xxv, 45: "Quamdiu non fecistis uni de minoribus his nec mihi fecistis" (note *ll.* 402-3 below).

*380* domunge ] deeming, judgment.

*385* god be swyche ] be of good sort.

*386* The anticlerical tinge of this line is conspicuous: Pantin (*op. cit.,* p. 238) has observed: "The candour and the capacity for criticism among preachers and writers of this period is remarkable. . . . It is very much to the credit of the men of the fourteenth century that it is they themselves who have supplied so liberally and openly the very materials with which modern historians have criticized them."

*390-409* Follows Matthew xxv, 33-40.

*406-8* ME manuals of pastoral instruction often contrast the joys of heaven with the torments of hell: e.g. *Speculum Christiani*, pp. 118-20, s.v. "De gaudiis celi, De penis inferni."

*414-18* These lines are similar to the ME "modus confitendi" formulas in which the penitent states that he has broken the Ten Commandments, misused the Five Bodily Senses, committed the Seven Deadly Sins, etc., and then begs the Deity for forgiveness: e.g., the ME *Form of Confession* in Horstmann, *Yorkshire Writers*, I, 182; "The Middle-English St. Brendan's Confession," ed. R. H. Bowers, Herrig's *Archiv*, CLXXV (1939), 40-49; Frank A. Patterson,

*The ME Penitential Lyric* (New York, 1911), No. 3 (the book has a very useful introduction to the subject). These formulas may be considered as instruction to the laity as to how they should conduct themselves when they confess to their priests, and properly undergo the three steps of contrition, confession, and penance (these steps are always explicated in the larger treatises on penance such as the ME *Book of Vices and Virtues*; or Chaucer's *Parson's Tale*, *ll* 107-8, which explicates: "Now shaltow understonde what is bihovely and necessarie to verray perfit Penitance. And this stant on three thynges: / Contricioun of herte, Confessioun of Mouth, and Satisfacioun"). J. De Ghellinck (*L'Essor de la littérature latine au XIIe siècle*, Brussels, 1954, II, 14) dryly remarks that confessional formulas served: "mener l'homme inculte et longtemps barbare à une saine et bienfaisante introspection de ses actes et de ses pensées." D. W. Robertson, Jr., has contributed several fine articles to this subject; see his "A Note on the Classical Origin of 'Circumstances' in the Medieval Confessional," *SP*, XLIII (1946), 6-14; "The Cultural Tradition of *Handlyng Synne*," *Speculum*, XXII (1947), 162 ff.

420 Treatises on the seven deadly sins are ubiquitous in ME; see Morton W. Bloomfield, *The Seven Deadly Sins* (East Lansing, Mich., 1952); Marie Gothein, "Die Todsünden," *Archiv für Religionwissenschaft*, X (1907), 416-84. One of the most vivid accounts is in *The Ancrene Riwle*, ed. M. B. Salu, chap. iv.

424 The line sounds proverbial: I have not traced a parallel.

425 flemes ] drives.

426 mas = makes.    fere ] companion.

428 oryual ] oriel window.

429 "In his own bawdry he is wholly shackled." Cf. William of Nassyngton, *Speculum Vitae* (Lansdowne MS 388, fol. 380$^r$): "The lechoure is the deuyles thrall / For in his baudom he is boundon all."

432-41 See note to *ll*. 321-22 above.

442-53 The most significant role that the Blessed Virgin Mary plays during the Middle Ages is that of the "mediatrix inter nos et Deum": since Christ died for man He ought to have mercy on him, and since Mary was His mother and typified mankind, He ought to be merciful when He looks on her. As a final argument, as she pleads with Him for mercy to mankind, she reveals her body: the efficacy of her body is based on the Song of Songs which long permeated devotional literature. Cf. Anselm, "Ora pro me Dei Genetrix" (*Ora-*

*tio* lviii, *PL,* CLVIII, 963): "Beata ubera tua quae lactaverunt Christum Dominum"; *Stanzaic Life of Christ, ll.* 9433-36:

> For the moder showes the son
> brest and pappes that soek he,
> whenne son is mynnet opon that wone
> on monkind he most haue pite.

These lines are introduced in the *Stanzaic Life* by St. Bernard, whose voluminous writings elaborating Marian doctrine are in his *Sermones in Cantica Canticorum, PL,* CLXXXIII)

**446-49** The poet also draws on the tradition of Jesus and Mary cooperating in pleading to the Father for mankind; cf. "Bonaventura," *Speculum Beatae Mariae (Opera,* Mainz, 1609, VI, 447ᵃ): "Filius nudato corpore Patri ostendit latus et vulnera, Maria Filio pectus et ubera. Non potest ullo modo fieri repulsa, ubi concurrant et perorant tanta charitatis insignia."

**448** warnyng ] prevention, withholding.

**449** MS tokynnyg.

**450** hete = eat, hence suck; the allusion appears to be to the miraculous milk of the BVM ("benedicta sit emanatio Virginei lactis tui"); cf. Hugh of St. Victor, *De Ubere Maternae Affectionis (PL,* CLXXVII, 812); Gower, *Mirour de L'Omme (Works,* ed. G. C. Macaulay, Oxford, 1889, I, 304), *ll.* 27418-20.

**452** qwame ] please, hence persuade.

**453** yeme ] snatch, protect.

**455** in stoundes ] once.

**460** siddele ] somewhat.

**461** mende af munde = mend of mind, hence reform, correct.

**469** drof ] derive.

**471** mede ] reward, share.

**472-73** Cf. *Speculum Christiani,* p. 1: "God es not louyde wythouten thyne neghbor. And thy neghtbor es not loued wyth-outen god"; Thomas Usk, *Testament of Love* (ed. W. W. Skeat), III, ix: "He that prayeth for other for him-selfe travayleth."

**475-76** This doctrine is based ultimately on John i, 17: "Quia lex per Moysen data est, gratia et veritas per Jesum Christum facta est." Harnack once noted (*History of Dogma,* trans. McGilchrist, London, 1899, vi, 276) that "the proposition of Irenaeus: Si non vere passus est, nulla gratia est, nulla gratia ei, cum nulla fuerit passio, formed the Alpha and Omega of Christian theology ... but as in itself it may mean many things, and, without definite interpretation, by no means guarantees the purity of the Christian religion — for what is grace?" Dom David Knowles, *The English Mystical Tradition* (London, 1961, p. 95), observes that "By the middle of the 14th century there was no sort of agreement in academic circles in England as to the nature of grace." Devotional literature understandably often hastens over many abstruse points of theology which are perhaps beyond the capacity of the spiritual director (or "souereyn goostly," as he is denominated in the ME *Book of Privy Counselling*, EETS OS No. 218, 1944, p. 153/4) to explicate in brief compass. The academic logomachia on grace during the first half of the fourteenth century is treated by Paul Vignaux, *Justification et prédestination au XIV^e siècle* (Paris, 1934); Gordon Leff, *Bradwardine and the Pelagians* (Cambridge, 1957).

477 ryche ] realm, hence heaven.

477-78 An allusion to the Beatific Vision, the doctrine that the righteous shall see God face to face in heaven. Based on I Corinthians xiii, 12: "Videmus nunc per speculum in aenigmate: tunc facie ad faciem," promulgated as dogma by Benedict XII in 1336 (Denzinger, *Enchiridion Symbolorum*, No. 530), it was a popular topic during the fourteenth century (see Paul Molinari, S.J., *Julian of Norwich*, London, 1958, pp. 109-10). But the doctrine is hazardous: it is contradicted by John i, 18: "Deum nemo vidit unquam"; hence it was debated in the schools: e.g., "Queritur utrum aliqua creatura possit videre Deum et cognoscere" (Assisi MS 158, fol. 47^r, cited in A. G. Little & F. Pelster, S.J., *Oxford Theology and Theologians, c A.D. 1282-1302*, Oxford, 1934, p. 108). Perhaps the most elaborate rendition of the BV is in Dante, *Paradiso*, xxxiii; certainly one of the most careful and balanced discussions is in Evelyn Underhill, *Mysticism* (13th ed.; London, 1940), pp. 267 ff. Dom David Knowles writes (*Religious Orders in England*, Cambridge, 1957), II, 86: "Christian tradition has always held that the BV, save in the altogether unique case of the human intelligence of Christ, is incompatible with mortal life." Recluses and mystics often claimed to have experienced visions — no doubt to the consternation of church officials: e.g., C. H. Talbot, *The Life of Christina of Markyate* (Oxford, 1959), p. 180: "Cumque respiceret ad altare vidit benignum Ihesum cum habitu et vultu pro propiciatur peccatoribus altario assistere." Preachers often mentioned the subject of the BV: e.g., *Middle English Sermons* (*EETS OS* No. 209, 1940), p. 114.

*482* hee se = eye see.
*483* here here = ear hear.
*501* won ] dwell.


## POEM 2

*2* A vivid depiction of falconry is contained in the ME *Parlement of the Thre Ages, ll.* 209-45, fully annotated in the recent *EETS* edition, *OS* No. 246 (1959), which refines the annotation in Gollancz's 1915 Oxford edition. The falcon figures in one of the loveliest of all Corpus Christi carols, the famous "He bare him up, he bare hym down," four versions of which are printed in R. L. Greene, *The Early English Carols*, No. 322 (Oxford, 1935).

*4* For the figure of the red meat used as a lure, cf. "The Seven Signs of Jesus' Love" in *The Tretyse of Loue (EETS OS* No. 223, 1951), p. 118/19-22: "The first signe of loue was shewed to vs in this, that he wold make of his precyous wounde the leure [i.e., lure] red and blody to call oure hertes, that be fleeing thoughtes ofte seaseth hem by fals loue vpon careyne of vayn creatures."

*10* reduce ] bring back.

*15-30* Raby records the legend that St. Francis received the stigmata on Mount Alvernus, the Five Wounds of Christ, "written on his fleshly members by the finger of the living God. Now in the minds of his followers he was perfectly transformed into the likeness of Christ . . . as he had imitated Christ in the deeds of his life so it behoved him to be conformed unto Him in the afflictions and sorrows of His passion" (*A History of Christian-Latin Poetry*, Oxford, 1927, p. 418). Woodcuts of St. Francis receiving the stigmata frequently appear in early printing; e.g., "Bonaventura," *La vita del glorioso san Francescho* (Milan: Zaroto, 1477; British Museum press mark: IB 25971).

*23, 25, 27* The tropological application of the nail, spear, blood, and water in these lines follows one of the four rules (i.e., the literal, allegorical, tropological, and anagogical) of interpreting Holy Writ; cf. "The thrid vnderstondyng is sence tropologik: that is whan a man redith a story that spekith moche of my3ti dedis or of gode worchyng and vnderstondith that he shuld haue strong gostli dedis of holy lyuyng that ben bitokened bi the stronge bodili dedis that this story spekith of" (Harley MS 2276, fol. 33ʳ, ed. R. H. Bowers, "A ME

54

Treatise on Hermeneutics," *PMLA*, LXV, 1950, 595). Widespread during the early part of the Middle Ages, the four-fold method of commenting on the Bible was often replaced in critical circles after the twelfth century (n.b., J. A. Robson, *Wyclif and the Oxford Schools*, Cambridge, 1961, p. 168) by the literal or historical method. Nevertheless the hermeneutic method continued to be used and abused by preachers and devotional poets in explicating Biblical symbols, hence the insistence of some modern medievalists that *all* medieval literature must be read according to symbolic exegesis, and the insistence of other modern medievalists that such procedure results in eisegesis, especially when it is applied to profane literature (for discussion of this see, *inter alia:* Morton W. Bloomfield, "Symbolism in Medieval Literature," *MP*, LVI, 1958-59, 73-81; *Critical Approaches to Medieval Literature*, ed. Dorothy Bethurum, New York, 1960; Elizabeth Salter, *Piers Plowman*, Oxford, 1962, pp. 66-70). To the best of my knowledge, few ME poems are strictly exegetical in procedure: a good example is the poem that calculates the distance that Christ "leaped" when He ascended into heaven (see Henry A. Person, *Cambridge Middle English Lyrics*, Seattle, 1953, No. 38; Montague R. James, A. *Descriptive Catalogue of the MSS in the Library of Corpus Christi College*, Cambridge, 1912, ii, 70).

## POEM 3

3 lofe thowt. Cf. A *Talking of the Loue of God*, ed. (from Bodleian MS 3938) Sister Salvina Westra (The Hague, 1950), p. 1: "This tretis is a talkyng of the loue of God. And is mad for to sturen hem that hit reden to louen him the more." Since love is a technical, operational term, which animates liturgical, devotional, and mystical literature over the centuries, it admits of no easy definition — especially since the basis of love is often assumed as in an enthymeme rather than asserted. Shepherd says: "No comprehensive study of this debate on love [the great theme of so much twelfth century writing], divine and profane, which continued over generations, has yet been made" (*Ancrene Wisse*: parts vi & vii, ed. Geoffrey Shepherd, New York, 1959, p. xlviii). Actually, Anders Nygren, *Agape and Eros* (trans. A. G. Hebert, New York, 1932-39), makes an attempt, but the work seems to me too contaminated by Lutheran prejudice to

treat medieval Catholic thought objectively; for a brief treatment, see S. K. Heninger Jr., "The Margarite-Pearl Allegory in Thomas Usk's *Testament of Love*," *Speculum*, XXXII (1957), 92-98. Love forms the rationale of the Christian life: Luke x, 27-28: "Diliges dominum deum tuum toto corde tuo, et ex tota anima tua, et ex omnibus viribus tuis, et ex omni menta tua: et proximum tuum sicut teipsum." The greatest manifestation of love was in the Sacrifice of Jesus. Human love was often thought of as an appetite of the conscious will (Hugh of St. Victor, *De Charitate*, PL, CLXXVI, 529: "Quid est Deum diligere? Habere velle"), which, when misdirected towards things of this world, becomes cupidity instead of charity (St. Augustine, *Sermo* cxxv, PL, XXXVIII, 694: "Qui amat saeculum amare Deum non potest. . . . Non occupetur amor tuus que potes ad Deum tendere, et inhaerere ei qui te creavit," a doctrine which medieval writers never tired of repeating, e.g., Hilton, *Scale of Perfection*, I.lxxi). If love arises from the will, it can be refined and perfected; hence the many medieval programs, or "ladders," instructing the Christian how to "perfect" his love for God through the stages of carnal, rational, to spiritual love (or through the stages of mystical purification, illumination, to unification); see É. Gilson, *Spirit of Medieval Philosophy*, chap. xiv, for a useful analysis of Cistercian spiritual exercise: "To love God is, in a way, to make God love Himself in us, as He loves Himself in Himself" (p. 300). But some mystics thought of love as a non-volitional manifestation of sanctified grace, or synderesis, basing such doctrine on James i, 1: "Omne datum optimum donum perfectum desursum est, descendens a Patre luminum, apud quem non est transmutatio, nec vicissitudinis obumbratio" (e.g., "He thorw his vnseable presence maketh miȝt & liȝt & loue and ȝiueth hit to thi soule" — *An Exposition of Qui Habitat and Bonum Est*, ed. Wallner Bjorn, Lund Studies in English, xxiii, 1954, p. 36, *l.* 13; cf. also James M. Clark, *Meister Eckhart*, Edinburgh, 1957, pp. 87-89). A good analysis of devotional love, which avoids hairline distinctions, may be found in Hilton's *Eight Chapters on Perfection* (ed. from Bibliothèque Nationale MS anglais 41, by Fumio Kuriyagawa, Tokyo, 1958).

7 loke ] locked; or past participle of look, hence focused.

8 lerus ] cheeks.

9 derne ] secret, private. Along with such terms as "privy," this one is frequently found in ME mystical writings which instruct an individual, not a community: Knowles notes (*Mystical Tradition*, p.

43): "It is a world [the fourteenth century England of the mystics] in which personal, individual problems and values are supreme, a world in which the kinds and degrees of love, divine and human, are matters of earnest debate.... It is a world quite different from the monastic world of the twelfth century." A. H. Thompson, *The English Clergy* (Oxford, 1947), p. 181, speaks of the "lonely blessedness and the blessed loneliness" of the Carthusian ideal.

11 A primary function of meditation, or of public preaching for that matter, is to stimulate the Christian to repent his sins: Eleanor Prosser (*op. cit.*, p. 25) thinks of "a typical Corpus Christi cycle as one vast sermon on repentence"; the mystical ME *Cloud of Unknowing* (*EETS OS* No. 218, 1944), p. 73, *ll.* 1-5, describes true meditation as "sodein conseites & blynde felyngs of theire owne wrechidnes, or of the goodnes of God, with-outyn any menes of redying or heryng comyng before, & with-outyn any specyal beholdyng of any thing vnder God."

18 Alluding to the state of self-effacement cherished by the mystics.

22 wyselokur ] more wisely; cf. *Piers Plowman*, B.xiii.343.

26 neynt ] nears, draws nigh.

31 Bisy the. The continual commands show the poet in the role of spiritual director; cf. the ME *Meditacyuns on the Soper of Our Lorde* (*EETS OS* No. 60, 1875), *ll.* 130, 136, 138, 170.

33-34 Devotional literature places stress on grace rather than works, and often implies that love is non-volitional since it comes from grace; see note to *l.* 3 above. Cf. the formula: "God ȝiue vs grace to serue God" (in a ME *Forma Confitendi* in Horstmann, *Yorkshire Writers*, II, 345), which reflects orthodox dogma (cf. Giles of Rome, *Errores Philosophorum*, ed. Josef Koch, Marquette, Wis., 1944, s.v. "errores Avicennae," No. 21: "Quod beatitudo nostra dependet ex operibus nostris").

40 dyhte ] prepared.

42 hafe drede. Alluding to Timor Domini (properly to be construed as "awe": one of the popular collections of sermons, the *Speculum Ecclesiae* of Honoré d'Auton, *PL*, CLXXII, 1067, contains a sermon enlarging on the theme: "Beati omnes qui timent Dominum"), which was regarded as the first of the seven gifts of the Holy Ghost (Isaiah xi, 2-3), since it prepares the Christian to receive the other gifts. It is constantly cited in ME didactic and pastoral literature: e.g., *Book of Vices and Virtues*, p. 117; *Hec sunt*

*dona vij Sancta Spiritus* in Cambridge University Library MS Ii.iv.9, fol. 189[r]: "in hym we owyn han drede and loue . . . (ed. R. H. Bowers, *MLN*, LXX, 1955, 250). The author of the *Pricke of Conscience* (*ll.* 9552-56) contends that perusal of his tract will stimulate "drede" in the reader, which is a frequent rationale of religious instruction. Hilton, *Goad of Love* (ed. Clare Kirchberger), vi, explains how the Passion "shineth to the sight of our soul a mirror" of the Seven Gifts of the Holy Ghost (p. 74).

55 ioynt ] joins, brings.

57-60 George Kane (*Middle English Literature*, London, 1951, p. 130) regards as inartistic devotional poems which aim at inducing a devout state of mind by merely an "express invitation extended by the poet to the reader to contemplate a particular religious subject and be devout accordingly." It is noticeable here that the poem omits all the narrative events prior to the Passion.

58 thore ] there.

63 The ME *Symbols of the Passion* (from British Museum Additional MS 22,029, ed. in *EETS OS* No. 46, 1881, pp. 170 ff) illustrate the significant items, with short captions underneath: *ll.* 69-72 read: "The crown of thorn on thi hed preste, / Thyn here to-tere, thy skyn to-breste. / Lord socowre me of synnes thys, / Of stlowthe and eke of Idylnes." The woodcuts in early printed books depicting the symbols of the Passion are of great interest: e.g., Pietro [Bernardini] da Lucca, *La arte del ben pensare e contemplare la passione del nostro signore Iesu Christo, con uno singolare trattato de imitar Christo* (Venice: Bindoni, 1541); the British Museum, *Guide to Medieval Antiquities* (1924, p. 4), states that the Passion was the most frequent subject for retable sets.

69 schene ] bright.

74 cos ] kiss, alluding to the kiss of Judas; cf. *Ludus Coventriae*, p. 265/997.

75 The detail of the gall and vinegar is constantly mentioned in accounts of the Passion; explicated as follows in the ME *Tretyse of Loue* (p. 88/10-12): "& thei offrid hym eysel & galle to thentent that he sholde dey more soner, but he wolde not drynke therof after that he had tasted it"; *Towneley* Pageant, No. 23 (p. 273, *l.* 481): "Thou shall haue drynke within a resse"; ME *Symbols of the Passion* (p. 185): "The vessel of aysylle and of galle, / Lord, kepe me from the synnys alle, / That to sowle ben venym, / That i be not poysynd ther-in."

*79-80* Cf. *Meditacyuns on the Soper of Our Lorde* (*ll.* 967-68):
"The euangelystes telle nat of thys doying, / For they my3te nat
wryte alle thyng." Speculation beyond the confines of the Four
Gospels, which is akin to the accretions which hagiographers ap-
pended to saints' lives (for which see Hippolyte Delehaye, S. J., *Les
légendes hagiographiques*, Brussels, 1905), was authorized by John
xx, 30: "Multa et alia fecit Jesus quae non sunt scripta in libro hoc,"
which is the often cited reading in the *Elucidarium*, the popular little
theological compendium of Honoré d'Auton (*PL*, CLXXII, 1127)
as opposed to the reading of the Clementine Vulgate: "Multa quidem et alia signa fecit Jesus in conspectu discipulorum suorum, quae
non sunt scripta in libro hoc." On variant readings and unauthorized
speculation, note Hans H. Glunz, *The History of the Vulgate in
England from Alcuin to Roger Bacon* (Cambridge, 1933), p. 213,
who, after noting that glosses sometimes introduced new readings,
says, "But with a pure form of the text nobody was concerned.
What mattered first of all was the sense of the passage, its true
reality. The text merely had to conform to it." See Leon E. Wright,
*Alterations in the Words of Jesus* (Cambridge, Mass., 1952) for
substantive variants arising from dogmatic, ethical, harmonistic, and
heretical motivations.

*81* onde ] envy.

*82* tho ] then, there.

*93* Numerical amplification beyond the traditional five wounds of
Christ is characteristic of accounts of the Passion that far exceed
mere rhetorical copia: cf. the ME *Mary's Lamentation to St. Bernard
on the Passion* (Horstmann, *Yorkshire Writers*, II. 281, *l.* 605):
"foure thowsand and sex hundreth woundes / dight thai on his sydes
ful sare." Note also the striking image of Rolle, *Meditations on the
Passion* (*English Writings*, ed. Allen, p. 35): "Efte swet Ihesu thy
body is like to a dufhouse. For a dufhouse is ful of holys, so is thy
body ful of woundes. And as a dove pursued of an hauk, yf she
mow cache an hool of hir hous she is siker ynowe, so, swet
Ihesu. . . ." The same amplification will be found in the iconography
of martyrdom: e.g., *The Martyrdom of St. Sebastian* by Antonio
and Piero Pollaiuolo in the National Gallery.

*99* Biblical chronology is here reversed.

*103* Cf. Peter of Poitiers, *Sentences* (*PL*, CCXI, 1209): "non
potuit nos meliori modo liberare quam per passionem Filii, quia non
potuit nos melius ad sui dilectionem trahere quam proprio Filio suo

non parcendo," an argument developed in the schools of Paris in the twelfth century to counter the query raised by the teachings of Abelard about the necessity of the Passion as the only possible means of the redemption of mankind.

*104* wreken ] avenge.

*111* MS fley3s.

*109-18* Cf. "Bonaventura," *Privity of the Passion* (Horstmann, *Yorkshire Writers*, I, 205): "Thane they nakynde hym agayne before all the pepill and rafe of bustously his clothes that were drye & bakene to his blissid body all-abowte hyme in his blyssede blode, and so they drew ofe the flesche & the skyne with-owttyne any pete. And sekerly this was a gret payne and a vnsufferabill, for there they renewede all his olde bryssynges & his dry wondes, and the skyne that before was lefte one hym, then was it alto-gedire rente of & cleuyde by his clothes."

*114* coled ] coagulated.

*116* redliche ] rudely, roughly.      breden ] ripped.

*120* y-schent ] reviled.

*127* wynne ] reach; the *Towneley* Pageant, No. 23, esp. *ll*, 120 ff., has these details, and is often considered the most vivid of ME accounts of the Passion in the mystery cycles.

*130* dreuen on. For the phrasing, cf. *Chester* Pageant No. 16, (*EETS ES* No. 115, 1914), *l.* 583: "now dryves on." Traditionally three nails were used: "Thorw eyther hond hi smyte a nayl; thorw the ffet the thridde" (*Southern Passion, l.* 1461), making four wounds; the piercing of His side by the spear of Longinus made the fifth. Rolle adds (*Meditations*, p. 24): "The nayles were blonte at the poynt, for thei schulde breste the skyn and the flesch."

*133* nele = ne will.

*135* senne = sin.

*147* senwe ] sinew.

*157* The detail of the mortice is lacking: cf. *Towneley* Pageant No. 23, 304: "let it into the mortase fall"; "Bonaventura," *Privity* (I, 206): "And aftere that they reysede vpe the crosse one Ende, as many as myghte ley hande one, & lett it fall downe in to a mortase of stone, was ordeyned therfore: and In this hevy fallynge all the ioyntes & cenowes of his blesside body braste in-sondire." A *Talking of the Loue of God* (p. 50): "A Ihesu now thei setten the cros in to the morteis. thi Ioyntes sturten out of lith. thi bones al to scateren. thi woundes ritten a brod for goled so wyde."

*166* Calvary was reserved for the execution of criminals, hence the Passion accounts prefix its denomination with such epithets as "stinking": e.g., "Bonaventura," *Privity* ( I, 205): "that stynkande place of Caluarye."

*169-82* Instead of the Mockery of Jesus by the Jews: "Litht doun of that harde tre, / King of Ieues yef thou be" (*Northern Passion,* EETS OS No. 183, 1930, *ll*, 1545-46); *Ludus Coventriae* Pageant, No. 32, *l.* 762: "heyl kyng of jewyse, yf thou be"; the poet shifts to the prophetic figura of Christ as a warrior, a figura brilliantly employed in *Piers Plowman* B.xviii.18-43 (for a discussion of which see Sister Marie Le May, *The Allegory of the Christ-Knight in English Literature,* Washington, 1932; and *PMLA,* XLVI, 1931, 155-69).

*172* gril ] horrible.

*176* feld ] probably foiled, rather than felt.

*180* Part of the Harrowing of Hell tradition (see *l.* 244 below; and note 38 of the Introduction above); many details from French texts are discussed by Jean G. Wright (*op. cit.*, pp. 83 ff.).

*186* tene ] injury, suffering.

*197* Cf. *Northern Passion* (*l.* 1643): "Alle was hire face bebed in blod."

*200* nas = he was.    chid = child.

*201* lomb. Cf. *Southern Passion* (*l.* 1431): "Euere stod the mylde lomb, and tholede al hare wille."

*209, 217* Cf. "Bonaventura," *Privity* (I, 203): "the wedire was colde."

*219* hosliche ] hostilely.

*223-43* The figura of Christ as a shepherd was commonplace; e.g., John x, 11: "Ego sum pastor bonus. Bonus pastor animam suam dat pro ovibus suis." Rabanus Maurus, *Allegoriae* (PL, CXII, 1022) correlates "pastus" with "instructio praelati." For discussion of ME instances of pastoral imagery see G. R. Owst, *Literature and Pulpit in Medieval England* (Cambridge, 1933), pp. 502-5; D. W. Robertson, Jr., and B. F. Huppé, *Piers Plowman and Scriptural Tradition* (Princeton, 1951), pp. 152-53.

*227* wederus ] storms.

*229* thorn ] hawthorne tree.

*232* MS brnge.    kende leswe = natural leese, hence own pasture (see *l.* 240 below).

*239* astrake ] strayed.

*243* aȝe ] again.

*253* MS The.

*255* Cf. *Stanzaic Life of Christ* (*ll.* 6093 ff.): "the furthe [point] was mon he offret fore / to make in Hym as one to be."

*257-80* According to legend Longinus was the blind Roman centurion who pierced Christ's side with a spear and subsequently had his sight restored by contact with the flowing blood. Hagiography opined that he was later converted at Cappadocia and became a monk — hence he became a monastic hero (see *Legenda Aurea*, I, 191). His legend was enormously popular during the Middle Ages and was variously interpreted; e.g., Ambrose: "quando de latere ejus aqua fluxit et sanguis, quo laetificavit animas universorum quia illo flumine lavit peccatum totius mundi" (*PL*, C, 986); *Southern Passion*, *ll.* 1641-44: "What by-toknede water and blod, that of Ihesus syde com? / That blod by-toknede him-sulf, and that water cristendom, / That withoute the swete blod, that he shadde on the treo / And withoute the water of cristendom, ne may no man y-saued beo." Many traditions are summarized in Bishop Brinton's sermon for Passion Sunday, 1374: "Vnus militum lancea latus eius aperuit et continuo exiuit sanguis et aqua (Johannis 19), sanguis in redempcionem et aqua in ablucionem. Et ecce quot de isto sanguine miracula contingerunt. Nam primo cecus illuminatur. Cum verum feruens Christi sanguis decurrens per lanceam tetigisset oculos laceantis, clare vidit, in Christum credidit, milicie cessit, instructus in fide per apostolos trigenta et octo annis monasticam vitam duxit, verbo et exemplo plures ad fidem conuertit et tandem pro Christo per martirum sanguinem suum fudit" (*The Sermons of Thomas Brinton, Bishop of Rochester* [1373-1389], ed. Sister Mary A. Devlin, *Camden Society Pub.*, 3rd series, lxxxv, 1954, pp. 159-60).

*259* breme ] fierce, brutal.

*281-84* The poet conflates the legend of the Spear of Longinus with the Sword of Symeon: Luke ii, 35: "et tuam ipsius animam pertransibit gladius ut revelentur ex multis cordibus cogitationes." Cf. *Ludus Coventriae*, No. 19, *ll.* 87-90, where Symeon prophesies both the Passion and the sword of sorrow that shall pierce the Blessed Virgin Mary: "Ffor whos passyon ther xal be-falle / Swych a sorwe bothe sharpe and smerte / that as a swerd perce it xalle / ȝevene thorwe his moderys herte."

*287* His frendes. Presumably Joseph of Arimathea and Nicodemus (John xix, 38-39). token hem to red ] betook themselves to counsel, hence, decided.

297 Only John xix, 25-27, mentions Mary's presence at the Crucifixion, hence Marian legend is in effect an accretion, but it permeates
Passion literature: e.g., "Bonaventura," *Privity* (I, 206): "whas sorow
and compassione was gretly the cause of encressyng of hir dere sones
passione, and the sones passione ekede the modire sorowe." Cf. the
ME *Talking of the Loue of God* (p. 54); *Towneley* Pageant, No. 23,
*ll.* 309 ff: "Alas! the doyll I dre / I drowpe / I dare in drede...."

299 MS nas.

299-300 In the *Towneley Pageant*, No. 23, *ll.* 400 ff; *Ludus Coventriae*, No. 32, *ll.* 906 ff., John tries to console Mary; in the Coventry
text he states the paradox: "had he not deyd we xuld to helle"
(*l.* 924).

301 Cf. Pseudo-Bernard, *De Passione Christi de Doloribus et
Planctibus Matris Ejus* (PL, CLXXXII, 1140): "Maria plorabat ipsa,
plorabant ambulantes cum ipse, plorabant multi venientes obviam
ei, sic usque deducitur a plorantibus plorantes quosque perventum
est ad domum Joannis."

306 kulte ] kissed. Cf. *Ludus Coventriae*, No. 34, *l.* 1145: "thi
blody face now I must kysse."

307 ful rine ] either, full salty,or, like rain.

308 MS mournyg.

316 helede ] covered.

321 stey3 ] ascended.

325 A shift to second person, and the inception of prayer, is likewise to be found in the ME *Meditations on the Life and Passion of
Christ* (EETS OS No. 158, 1921, *ll.* 2027-28): "Lord that art so lef
and dere, / Dispise not my pore preiere"; and the liturgical incanta-
tion with which *ll.* 325, 327, 329, and 331 reverberate, recalls Rolle's
iterated thanksgiving for the Sacrifice: "Swete Jhesu, I thanke the
and I 3elde the graces..." (*Meditations on the Passion*, pp. 19 ff).

333 ryue ] manifold.

344 Cf. Matthew xxvii, 50: "emisit spiritum"; Mark xv, 37: "exspiravit"; Luke xxiii, 46: "exspiravit"; John xix, 30: "tradidit spiritum." The metaphysical problem of the relation of the body and the
soul implied in *l.* 344 was so difficult that ME writers tended to
ignore it: e.g., Gower, *Mirour de L'Omme*: "De ceste vie il se des-
joynt: / Mais lors tieus signes desmoustra, / Qe nuls par droit se
doubtera / Q'il n'est ove dieu le piere joynt" (*ll.* 28750-52); *Towneley* Pageant, No. 23: "ffader of heuen, in to thyn hende / I betake
my saull!" (*ll.* 591-92). *Ludus Coventriae*, No. 33, represents a bodi-

less spirit in the character of Anima Christi: "I am the sowle of cryst jhesu ... my body is ded the jewys it slew," who conducts the Harrowing of Hell prior to the Resurrection (*ll.* 979, 981). Related is the general problem of the relation of the body and the soul; see É. Gilson on the subject of Christian anthropology in *The Spirit of Medieval Philosophy* (pp. 167 ff); R. W. Ackerman, "The Debate of the Body and the Soul and Parochial Christianity," *Speculum,* XXXVII (October, 1962), 540 ff.

*349, 354* See note to *ll.* 33-34 above.

*355-56* Richard B. Sewell, *The Vision of Tragedy* (New Haven, 1959), p. 52, writes: "Neither the Greeks nor Job knew the deep Christian consciousness of sin or the Christian's need for constant self-examination. Though Job approached this state, it took a catastrophe to turn his eyes inward: he never knew the sense of one's love being infinitely inadequate return for Christ's love in dying for man."

*359* stoke ] stuck, hence, rooted.

*361* redlich ] readily, promptly.

*365* Contrast the extravagance of Rolle (*Meditations,* p. 26): "I wolde among the dede, that lyn styngynge fouly, lay me flat on the grounde, and netherere ʒyf I my ʒte, the vertu and the grace to kepe of thi blood. Thennes wyl I not ryse ne non gate flytte, tyl I be with thi precyous blood bycome al reed ... and my soule softyd in that swete bath."

*366* strong ] painful, bitter.

*367* qued = cwed ] evil.

*373* be ryʒt of rest ] Construe: according to any claim to peace of mind; or according to any feeling of self-righteousness.

*382* MS stong.

*386* grace. Why God granted grace to some and withheld it from others was usually considered a mystery: e.g., William of Shoreham, *Poems* (EETS ES No. 86, 1902), No. vii: "Ac wy he graunteth grace to one, / And soche and otheren graunteth none, / Segge ich ne kanne; / Bote thet hys priuete / Of hys domes in equyte, / Wyth wyl to thanne" (*ll.* 511-16). And it would be the height of presumption to probe this mystery, to seek forbidden knowledge and question God's purposes: e.g., the ME *Cato's Distiches,* ii (EETS OS No. 117, 1901, *ll.* 329-32): "Aske not what god wol do / Of the world bi cas / Withouten the and othur alle / He mai worche with his gras."

*390* An allusion to Dismas, the good thief who was crucified on the right side of Jesus, and to whom Our Lord said: "hodie mecum eris in Paradiso" (*Luke* xxiii, 43). He often appears in ME charms against thieves; see Curt F. Bühler, "Three ME Prose Charms from Harley MS 2389," *N&Q*, n.s. IX (February, 1962), 48.

397 pouste ] dominion.

398 Cf. the sentiment: "For al this werd with-outen the ne sal me maken blithe" (Carleton Brown, *Religious Lyrics of the XIVth Century*, Oxford, 1924, No. 64, *l.* 12).

# UNIVERSITY OF FLORIDA MONOGRAPHS